A USER'S GUIDE TO PILOT

A USER'S GUIDE TO PILOT

john starkweather

A SPECTRUM BOOK

Prentice-Hall, Inc.
Englewood Cliffs, New Jersey 07632

Library of Congress Cataloging in Publication Data

Starkweather, John.
    A user's guide to PILOT.

    "A Spectrum Book."
    Includes index.
       1. PILOT (Computer program language)   I. Title.
QA76.73.P54S73 1985   001.64′24   84-26645
ISBN 0-13-937755-7
ISBN 0-13-937748-4 (pbk.)

1 2 3 4 5 6 7 8 9 10

ISBN 0-13-937755-7

ISBN 0-13-937748-5 {PBK.}

Bookware® is a registered trademark of Prentice-Hall, Inc.

Editorial/production supervision by Lori L. Baronian
Manufacturing Buyer: Gary Orso
Cover design © 1985 by Hal Siegel

This book is available at a special discount when ordered in
bulk quantities. Contact Prentice-Hall, Inc., General
Publishing Division, Special Sales, Englewood Cliffs, N.J. 07632

Prentice-Hall International (UK) Limited, *London*
Prentice-Hall of Australia Pty. Limited, *Sydney*
Prentice-Hall Canada Inc., *Toronto*
Prentice-Hall Hispanoamericana, S.A., *Mexico*
Prentice-Hall of India Private Limited, *New Delhi*
Prentice-Hall of Japan, Inc., *Tokyo*
Prentice-Hall of Southeast Asia Pte. Ltd., *Singapore*
Whitehall Books Limited, *Wellington, New Zealand*
Editora Prentice-Hall do Brasil Ltda., *Rio de Janeiro*

Contents

Preface

PILOT is a specialized computer language for developing conversational scripts. It provides an easy way to specify what information you would like the computer to present to its user and how it should deal with responses that the user may make. Although it has been primarily used to develop sequences of instruction and testing, PILOT programs have also been used for a variety of other conversational tasks, such as gathering data or providing information.

When used as an authoring language for writing computer assisted instruction lessons, PILOT lets you decide how you want lesson material presented to a student and how you want the student's response evaluated. You can include elements of assistance when the students' responses indicate that they are having difficulty.

This book has three parts: a tutorial introduction, examples of applications of PILOT programming, and appendices of supplemental information. The five chapters of Part One provide an introduction to PILOT and prompt the reader to develop simple program segments. Beginning with Chapter Two, a brief PILOT program provides a quiz on the contents of each chapter and at the same time demonstrates use of the PILOT elements just described.

Chapter Three describes the statement types that make up the core of PILOT, Chapter Four presents some common extensions to the basic language, and Chapter Five discusses techniques for the development of more complex programs.

Part Two presents and discusses programming examples of different applications of PILOT, each with PILOT code that can be adapted to similar uses.

Chapters Six through Nine have examples of giving and gathering information, quizzes and examinations, and a simulation of a problem situation.

The appendices provide a history of PILOT and its initial descriptive standards, a comparison of some current PILOT systems, a glossary of technical terms, and the expected correct responses to quizzes in Chapters Two through Five.

As is true of most computer languages, there are somewhat differing versions of PILOT, with departures from the standard and extensions to the language. These departures are not great, and Appendix Three provides information for making changes that may be necessary. In order to get the greatest benefit from this book, you should supplement it with the programmer's reference manual for your version of PILOT and actually run the programs listed here.

ACKNOWLEDGMENTS

The U.S. Office of Education (through grant OE 6-10-131) supported the development of COMPUTEST, the predecessor to and first version of PILOT.

The U.S. Public Health Service (through extramural grant LM-01843 of the National Library of Medicine) supported the development of PILOT on a single user machine, the Datapoint 1200.

The National Library of Medicine (via contract LO-467378-06 also supported development of PILOT for the 8080 microprocessor.

Staff and students of the Dixie Elementary School District in Marin County, California were important early participants.

Colleagues at the University of California at San Francisco Computer Center were heavily involved in the development of

PILOT. Major early contributors were Martin Kamp and Richard Karpinski.

Many other members of the faculty, staff, and student body at UCSF assisted through their use of PILOT and their reactions to interactions with PILOT.

GETTING
ACQUAINTED
WITH PILOT AND
COMPUTER
PROGRAMMING

Introduction

WELCOME TO PILOT

You are about to learn a system that will put you in control of many useful computer functions; in particular, those that allow the computer to assist with teaching, training, testing, and data gathering. This book will lead you step by step while you practice all the major operations of the PILOT language. The tutorial guide starts in Chapter 2, where you will discover that you can rapidly obtain useful results with the basic functions of core PILOT. These basic functions exist in all versions of PILOT, although there are variations in additional features. Appendix II describes some of the variations in available PILOT systems.

For many educational applications, you may find that these basic functions are all you need. The use of core PILOT is often learned within one or two hours—much can be accomplished with this simple portion of the system. The beginning chapters of this book start with basic functions and prompt you to obtain immediate results. Later chapters give examples of more complex programs and provide exercises for practice with many advanced features.

WHAT IS PILOT?

You have probably received many letters, bills, and reports that were produced by computers. If you have ever used an automatic teller at a bank, made an airline reservation, or even used a telephone, you have interacted with a computer program. Perhaps you've used a word processor or a memory typewriter—whatever your occupation, it would be difficult to avoid using computers.

PILOT Uses the Computer for Conversation

You may have wondered what you need to know in order to direct a computer to perform some new tasks that you require. Perhaps you have a student you would like to instruct, a customer you would like to help, or an employee you would like to train, and you wonder if you could have the computer assist you in such an assignment. In other words, you would like to PILOT the computer to act on your behalf in communicating with someone else. The PILOT programming system will give you a way to do this by providing you with a set of tools that you can easily understand and put to immediate use.

PILOT gets its name not only from the general goal of turning you into a computer pilot but also as a reminder of just some of the uses to which it has been put: Each letter represents the words *Programmed Inquiry Learning Or Teaching.*

PILOT Can Play the Role of a Human Helper

Because the PILOT system was developed to be interactive and conversational, it allows the computer to play the role of a human helper. A PILOT program can act as a tutor or consultant; it can be the giver of tests and examinations; it can ask questions and prompt the collection of data; and it can describe and assist in the learning of other computer systems.

WHY USE PILOT INSTEAD OF OTHER PROGRAMMING LANGUAGES?

The uses for PILOT just cited suggest that PILOT is oriented more toward the use of language than to solving number problems. If your primary interest is calculation, computation, statistics, or accounting, other computer systems and programming languages will likely fit your needs better than PILOT. However,

PILOT makes it easy and natural to accomplish some of the conversational operations that you may be interested in producing or developing.

PILOT is a widely used *author language* for the creation of computer-assisted instruction. It is a collection of specialized programming tools for the development of computer dialog. PILOT is not an *authoring system* with prearranged formats ready for instructional use, though it can be used to create a variety of such formats. PILOT is designed to have an exceedingly simple entry level and immediate feedback for a novice program author who wishes to present information and evaluate a user's response. Because of this, PILOT has been used as a first introduction to computers, and has been especially successful with young children.

The features of PILOT can be combined with the advantages of other programming languages. Sometimes there are problems that require much explanation, questioning, and collection of data as a preliminary to extensive computation. PILOT can be combined with other systems to make such an introductory section easy to program. Major computational tasks can be transferred to other systems at the appropriate time, after data has been collected. Improvement of the interactive portion of such a system is important: PILOT makes it easier for the computer to prompt the user and explain what is desired. The user is in direct control, knowing that assistance is nearby. Although these features can be provided when using other computer languages, they are usually much more difficult than the PILOT system: It takes greater thought and effort on the part of the developer to program conversational interaction with a general-purpose computer language.

THE ELEMENTS OF CONVERSATION

Most conversations between two people involve an alternation of some simple, basic elements. Each person needs to present information or ask questions; each needs to listen and accept answers. As a third and more complex element, each person needs to evaluate what is seen or heard and respond differently as a result of that evaluation. These three elements describe the major core mechanisms of PILOT. In order to remove any ambiguity about what the computer is expected to do, code letters followed by a colon are used to indicate when the computer is to perform one of these functions. These are called PILOT *statements*.

PILOT Can Present Information or Ask a Question

The symbol T: is followed by *text* (information or a question) that is to be *typed* or displayed by the computer. For example, the following line in a PILOT program:

```
T: Hello there, whoever you are.
```

will cause the computer to type or display:

```
Hello there, whoever you are.
```

All words, numbers, punctuation, or spaces following the colon are displayed. There is no functional difference involved in arranging for the computer to ask a question. Thus, the following:

```
T: What is your name?
```

will cause the computer to type or display:

```
What is your name?
```

exactly copying the line of text that follows T:.

The T: (Type) statement is simply repeated in order to display more than one line of text. For example:

```
T: Two tractors can together plow a field
T: in eight hours.
T: How long will it take three tractors to
T: plow a field of the same size if all
T: tractors operate at the same speed?
```

will cause the computer to display

```
Two tractors can together plow a field
in eight hours.
How long will it take three tractors to
plow a field of the same size if all
tractors operate at the same speed?
```

PILOT Can Accept Answers
and Try to Find Meaning

The A: statement directs the computer to *accept* an *answer* from the user. The M: statement is followed by words or elements of text for which a *match* will be attempted within the text of the latest answer. For example:

A:

M: FRED

will cause the computer to *accept* an *answer* from the console keyboard and to look for a *match* with "FRED".

PILOT Can React Differently
to Different Answers

In order to take different actions in response to different answers, the letters Y or N may be added to the code letters in PILOT statements. These letters are *conditioners* that cause the statement to be effective or not as a result of the success of the last attempted match. If a match was found (YES), then a statement such as TY: will operate but TN: will not; if a match was not found (NO), then TN: will operate but TY: will not.

Let's look at an example of PILOT coding for a conversational interchange. For the moment, assume that PILOT is in operation and that you have created and stored a brief PILOT program within the memory of the computer. PILOT displays the word "READY", indicating that it is waiting for a command. If you type the command "list", PILOT will display the program. (This means that you will see the sequence of PILOT instructions already prepared.) If you type the command "run", PILOT will run the program. (This means that the computer will obey the sequence of instructions and you will see the effect of their operation.)

What the PILOT user types will be shown in boldface to distinguish it from what is typed by PILOT. Here is the program as it would be displayed by the version called Nevada PILOT, which runs on a variety of microcomputers using the CP/M operating system.

8

```
user    ->  list
PILOT   ->  T: Is it usually colder in the summer or in the winter?
PILOT   ->  A:
  "         M: winter
  "         TY: That's true most places.
  "         TN: You must be thinking of an unusual place.
```

Here is the result of running the program:

```
user    ->  run
PILOT   ->  Is it usually colder in the summer or in the winter?
user    ->  In the winter.
PILOT   ->  That's true most places.
PILOT   ->  READY
```

I can run the program again and provide a different response:

```
user    ->  run
PILOT   ->  Is it usually colder in the summer or in the winter?
user    ->  I'll say summer.
PILOT   ->  You must be thinking of an unusual place.
PILOT   ->  READY
```

Let's review the listed program and see what caused the computer to respond as it did. A T: statement prompts the computer to type (display) whatever follows the colon. In this case, it is a question. Next, the A: statement then accepts an answer from the user. Following that, M: attempts to match the word "winter" with any portion of the response. If a match was found (yes), then the response "That's true most places." was typed because TY: causes display only when a match has occurred. If a match is not found (no), then the alternate response occurred because TN: causes display only when a match has *not* occurred. The simple codes (T:, A:, and M) at the front of each line indicate the basic conversational elements and the extra letter Y or N *conditions* operation according to whether a match has occurred.

Here is another example:

```
user    ->  list
PILOT   ->  T: I'm feeling chilly.
  "         T: Do you mind if I close the window?
```

```
PILOT ->   A:
   "        M: no
   "        TY: Ok, I'll close it.
   "        TN: Then perhaps you could bring me a sweater.


user ->    run
PILOT ->    I'm feeling chilly.
PILOT ->    Do you mind if I close the window?
user ->    No, go ahead.
PILOT ->    Ok, I'll close it.
PILOT ->    READY


user ->    run
PILOT ->    I'm feeling chilly.
PILOT ->    Do you mind if I close the window?
user ->    I'd rather you didn't
PILOT ->    Then perhaps you could bring me a sweater.
PILOT ->    READY
```

T: is first used to present information; then it is used to ask a question. A: is next used to accept an answer from the user of the computer. M: causes a search for the word "no" in the answer. This causes a switch to be set that will affect the operation of the Y and N conditioners. If "no" is found in the answer, then a match has occurred and the Y conditioner will be effective.

The following two statements make use of these conditioners to cause a choice of two possible responses. In each case, the response is typed or not typed, depending on whether a match with "no" was found or not found. TY: means type the following if a match was found; TN: means type the following if a match was *not* found. Note that this choice has nothing to do with the content of what was being looked for. If "no" was typed, then a match will be found and TY: will be effective even though the content of the answer was "no". The way this question was written required that PILOT look for a match with "no". Having done so, it is the success or failure of the match that will determine whether TY: (success) or TN: (failure) will display its contents.

COMPUTER REQUIREMENTS FOR PILOT OPERATION

PILOT Goals Relate to Elements of a Computer

The major elements of a computer can be described paralleled to the elements of conversation that we wish to put into operation. We will likely use a *terminal* for typing or displaying information—it will look like a sophisticated typewriter with a television screen above the keyboard. This is the device on which the T: statement will type information. The keyboard of the terminal will be the usual source of information for the A: statement. The display device and keyboard unit is often called the *console.*

To create a PILOT program, we make use of whatever facility the computer system has for the creation of text files. Some versions of PILOT accept the entry of PILOT statements directly while others require the use of an external program called an *editor* in order to prepare the program text. A PILOT program consists of lines of text that can be interpreted by PILOT to cause specific actions of the computer. The way you create the program text is unimportant as long as it conforms to the rules of PILOT.

The computer has a memory used for storing both the sequence of instructions that we wish the computer to carry out and also data that may be used by those instructions. When we create a PILOT program with an editor, the program text exists in computer memory. Most of the time that PILOT is in operation, the program is in the computer's memory. In most computers, the memory contents are lost when the computer is turned off. We can, however, save information in a more permanent form by creating a *file* on another device, often a magnetic disk unit.

The computer has a logic unit that can make comparisons and take different actions depending upon what is found. It is this capability that gets used when we write an M: statement and then make use of the results of an attempted match in order to take different actions in response to different answers.

PILOT ALLOWS YOU TO DESIGN
COMPUTER OPERATION FOR OTHERS

Since you are undoubtedly already a user of computer programs written by others (such as your department store bill), you have experienced the differences in the ability of different computers and different computer programs to understand and be responsive to your needs. You have perhaps been limited to one side of the conversation and have not been able to control the sequence of operation. PILOT will make it possible for you to play the other role and develop programs that are increasingly able to meet needs that you define. You will soon find that users' responses are sometimes difficult to predict. Don't be surprised if you find it necessary to enlist the help of trial users of your program in order to collect sample responses. You will then begin to see the need for some further functions that give you additional capability beyond the simple examples mentioned so far. The PILOT system has many additional tools that will prove useful when you run into such problems.

SUMMARY

What Can PILOT Do for You?

PILOT can assist you with computer-based teaching, training, testing, and data gathering.

PILOT will provide you with a set of easily used tools for conversational assistance in reaching your goals.

PILOT can play the role of a human assistant.

PILOT functions can assist in the use of other computer programs.

PILOT Fundamentals

T: instructs the computer to *type* or display whatever follows on the same line.

A: instructs the computer to *accept* and answer.

M: causes an attempt to *match* elements of the answer.

The letters Y or N cause PILOT instructions to be obeyed (Y) or not (N) depending on whether the last M: statement found a match (Yes) or did not find a match (No).

Computer Fundamentals

You will most likely use a computer terminal for the display of information. Display may be caused by PILOT T: statements. The PILOT program must exist in computer memory before it can operate. Before the computer is turned off, the program must be saved in a more permanent form. The logic unit of the computer makes comparisons such as those prompted by PILOT M: statements, and the results can cause different actions to occur (such as different displays).

Writing Your First
PILOT Program

PILOT versions will differ in some details and some of the differences will depend on the particular computer system that you are using. Special characteristics of some available PILOT systems are described in Appendix II. One way that PILOT systems differ is in the method used to create a PILOT program. The PILOT system is an interpreter of a sequence of PILOT statements; it is not affected by the style of the text of the statements. There are many programs for creating and editing text that can be used to prepare PILOT statements. Some versions of PILOT provide special editors for this purpose; for example, the Apple version. The Atari PILOT uses the same program entry and editing method as its computer provides for the BASIC language. It therefore requires line numbers for editing, even though PILOT operation makes no use of line numbers. The Nevada PILOT provides a visual editor that is especially convenient because it is immediately available to the program author.

While you are learning to use PILOT, it is helpful to have a system that contains a built-in editor so that you can quickly make a new program or make changes to an existing one. In any case, your first assignment will be to learn how to use the editor or the editor portion of PILOT in order to create PILOT program material.

I'm going to assume that you have been able to put PILOT into operation. If you are using Nevada PILOT, you will see the word "READY" on the screen. There is a limited number of direct commands that can be used at this time. If you type "?" and press "RETURN", some PILOT versions will display a list of commands. (Most of the time, you should press "RETURN" after you

15

finish typing a command or a line of text. The computer won't respond to what you've typed until you've pressed "RETURN".)

At this point, PILOT is in the *immediate* mode, waiting for one of the immediate commands to be entered. At any one time, PILOT is in one of three operating modes; the other two are *run* mode and *edit* mode (if available). In run mode, what happens is under control of a previously prepared PILOT program, while in edit mode, we can develop or change the text of a PILOT program. When PILOT is in the immediate mode, the word "READY" is displayed. PILOT will not know what to do with words that are not on the list of immediate commands: These words will be ignored or questioned as an error.

Now let's make use of the editor to prepare text for PILOT to interpret. If you are using Nevada PILOT, type "edit" or "EDIT" (either upper- or lower-case letters) in order to enter the edit mode. The screen will clear and you will be able to create and store text that may turn out to be a PILOT program. With other PILOT systems you may need to use an editor external to the PILOT system.

You can use the editor to create any kind of text, but if the text doesn't follow the rules for PILOT, it won't operate as a PILOT program. Just to see what happens, type "Hello, PILOT" and then leave the edit mode. (In the Nevada PILOT, press the letter K while holding down the key marked "CTRL".)

You are now back in the immediate mode where you will see the word "READY". The text you created is stored in the computer memory. You can view it by typing "list", and you can see how PILOT reacts to it by entering the run mode. Now type "run" (remember to press "RETURN"). PILOT will display what you wrote and then inform you that it is an unrecognizable PILOT statement.

Let's see if we can get PILOT to type what we want without complaint. If you enter the edit mode again (get the word READY on the screen and then type "edit") you should again see what you wrote, which enables you to make changes. Use the editor to change "Hello, PILOT" to "T: Hello PILOT". Either retype the line or use the editor to insert T: at the beginning of the existing line. Then leave the edit mode and try "run" again. You will see "Hello PILOT" and there will be no complaint. If you try some other combinations, you will find that whatever follows T: (or t:) on the same line will be typed, that is, displayed on the screen. The symbol T: alone will result in a blank line. It's a good idea to type some more lines, each line beginning with T:. For example, use the editor to create text similar to the following lines of PILOT statements:

```
T:Hello, PILOT
T:My name is Jim  (fill in your own name)
T:
T:Now I know how to type information on the screen
T:This isn't much of a program.
```

Now exit from the editor and type "run" to PILOT. You will see all four lines.

```
user ->    run
PILOT ->   My name is Jim
  "
  "            Now I know how to type information on the screen
  "            This isn't much of a program.
```

One of the other immediate commands is "LIST". Try typing "LIST" when you are in the immediate mode. You will see that everything you prepared with the editor is displayed, including the PILOT codes. LIST will display everything, regardless of whether or not it might operate as a PILOT program.

```
user ->    list
PILOT ->   T:Hello, PILOT
  "            T:My name is Jim
  "            T:
  "            T:Now I know how to type information on the screen
  "            T:This isn't much of a program.
```

PILOT is a kind of computer system called an *interpreter*. When we type "run", we are asking the computer to interpret information that it will find in a part of computer memory called the *program space*. If what it finds there follows the rules of PILOT, then it carries out the instructions of the PILOT statements, one after another. If the rules are not followed, then you will see a complaint, such as "*UNRECOGNIZED PILOT STATEMENT". All PILOT statements begin with one or more characters followed by a colon, so the absence of a colon will immediately be cause for complaint.

The edit mode puts you in control of the contents of the program space and lets you make changes to it. Thus, you were able to change your text to make it a legal PILOT statement. There is also a way to make PILOT interpret a single PILOT statement when you are in the immediate mode. Recall that there are a limited number of immediate commands, such as "RUN" or "EDIT", that can be given in this mode. The Nevada PILOT lets you see a list of them if you type "?". The immediate mode is sometimes called the *direct* or *executive* mode because instructions are directly executed when typed.

The word "command" will be used to mean a direct instruction to the computer—it will usually be used in immediate mode. The word "statement" will be used to mean a line in a program that is deferred in its action. Statements are saved in an area of memory called the *program space,* and they form a PILOT program. Statements become active when the program is "run"; they are obeyed one after the other. When there are no more statements for PILOT to interpret, there is an automatic return to immediate mode.

So far, we have described three commands: EDIT, RUN, and LIST. In addition, we have written some T: statements and *run* them. If we wish to exit from PILOT and return to the operating system, we type "BYE". It is amazing how many words are used for this purpose in various different computer systems: "QUIT", "EXIT", "LOGOUT",and "SYSTEM" are just a few. In the Nevada PILOT, if you forget what your choices of immediate commands are, just type "?" and select from the list.

```
user ->    ?
PILOT ->   LOAD GET RUN DIR BYE INFO
PILOT ->   EDIT SAVE LIST NEW VNEW CREATEF KILLF SET
```

Using Other PILOT Statements
as Immediate Commands

In the Atari PILOT, if you type a PILOT statement without a line number, it will be interpreted with immediate results. For example, if you type "T:Hello", you will see the result "Hello". When we get to more complicated PILOT statements, you may find this a useful way to test what a statement will do. In the Nevada PI-LOT, this immediate and direct operation is accomplished by typing "\" (a backward slash) before the statement you wish to use. The same example will look like this:

```
user ->    \T:Hello
PILOT ->   Hello
```

The backward slash will force immediate interpretation of a PILOT statement not only when you are in immediate mode, but also when you are in run mode and are about to give a response to an A: statement. This feature is particularly helpful during the course of program development and testing. As a program author, you may be running your program for test purposes and wish to change the value of certain program variables or shift operation to another location in the program. You can do this by using immediate interpretation of appropriate PILOT statements. If the backward slash is followed immediately by "RE-TURN", there will be an immediate shift from run mode to immediate mode, with abandonment of further program operation.

ENTERING AND EDITING
YOUR FIRST EXAMPLE PROGRAM

Here's one way that you can be friendly with the user of your program. Using the editor available to you, create the following brief PILOT program:

```
user ->    list
PILOT ->   T: Hello, what is your first name?
   "       A:
   "       T: I'm glad to meet you.
```

With Nevada PILOT, which contains a built-in editor, type "edit". The screen will clear and and you can type the three lines as shown. Then press the proper keys (CTRL and K) to leave the editor. Here we have created one side of a conversation. A question will be asked, an answer will be accepted, and then a comment will be made. We have defined what the computer will do. It will be up to the user of the program to provide the other side of the conversation. You can play that role by putting PILOT into operation and responding to the program when it runs. You can now type "run" to put the program into operation. This is sometimes called *executing* the program.

```
user ->     run
PILOT ->    Hello, what is your first name?
user ->     John
PILOT ->    I'm glad to meet you.
PILOT ->    READY
```

Changing the Example
to Recognize Known Names

It seems obvious that this program accepts an answer from its user but has no ability to make use of it. Let's modify the program a bit and assume that the program author would like to know whether the program will be dealing with certain specific people. Just for example, we will assume that the author has something special to say to John, Jim, or Sally and that it makes no difference which one is the current user.

```
user ->     list
PILOT ->    T: Hello, what is your first name?
   "        A:
   "        M: John, Jim, Sally
   "        TY: Perhaps I know you already.
   "        TN: I'm glad to meet you.
```

You see here that the M: statement can have more than one item. Each item is listed after the colon and separated by commas (the Apple PILOT separates items with an exclamation mark). Any one of the items will count as a match when compared against the answer given by the user of our program. If you put PILOT into operation, you will see a different result if you answer with or without one of these names.

```
user ->     run
PILOT ->    Hello, what is your first name?
user ->     John
PILOT ->    Perhaps I know you already.
```

20

Now let's run it again, entering a different name.

```
user  ->    run
PILOT ->    Hello, what is your first name?
user  ->    Bill
PILOT ->    I'm glad to meet you.
```

We will now claim that our program is somewhat more friendly, at least for John, Jim, and Sally. It wouldn't look different to anyone else, as we can see from the last run in which we entered "Bill". Now let's try a somewhat different route to indicating recognition of the person who is responding to the program. In the first version, the answer given by our user was accepted but not remembered or used at all. In our most recent version, the answer given was remembered only long enough to look for a match with the particular first names listed in the M: statement.

SAVING AND USING A NEWLY PROVIDED NAME

PILOT has a way to remember the response in a more permanent fashion so that it can be used at a later time. This requires providing a reference name under which to file the response so that it can be retrieved later on. Since the entry we are going to store is collected as a string of characters and and the characters may be variable depending on the entry, the reference name is called a *string variable*. String variables start with a symbol of a dollar sign ($) and have up to ten characters to form their names. (The rules for Apple PILOT are more complicated. See Appendix II.) Keep in mind that the string variable is just a name under which we are filing whatever it is our user answers. In this case, the string variable could be "$name" or "$answer1" or any other name we choose. Let's try an example:

```
user  ->    list
PILOT ->    T: Hello, what is your first name?
  "         A: $entry
  "         T: I'm glad to meet you, $entry.
```

Now we have stored the answer given under the label under the string name "$entry". When the program runs, the second T:

statement will differ as "$entry" is replaced by the actual response from the program user.

```
user  ->     run
PILOT ->     Hello, what is your first name?
user  ->     John
PILOT ->     I'm glad to meet you, John.
```

And now we'll run it again, entering a different name.

```
user  ->     run
PILOT ->     Hello, what is your first name?
user  ->     Bill
PILOT ->     I'm glad to meet you, Bill.
```

We now have a choice about what to do with the entry of text information by a user. We can simply accept an answer, look for various possibilities in the answer, and take different actions depending upon what we find; or we can cause the creation of a string variable, giving it a name by which it will be known. The entry of the user will remain available under that name for later use unless we accept new information under the same string variable name. Such action will obliterate the former contents.

Collecting and Saving Other Information

In some applications, we wish to use a conversational interchange in order to collect data in a more permanent fashion. For this we ask PILOT to open a data file to store information on magnetic disks. This creates a file which we can later retrieve and perhaps use as data in other separate programs. By using this method, we write interactive questionnaires that can ask appropriate questions, skip over unnecessary sections, and collect information in a consistent way that will be machine readable for input to other systems.

SUMMARY

PILOT has three operating modes:

The immediate mode takes immediate action in response to a command. Available commands may be seen by typing "?".

The run mode follows instructions of PILOT statements in the program space, obeys each PILOT statement in turn, and returns to the immediate mode when finished. If PILOT cannot interpret a line of text, the line will be displayed with the message "*UNRECOGNIZED PILOT STATEMENT".

The edit mode accepts entry of text into the program space and allows changes to existing program text.

In the immediate mode, or during response to an A: statement, PILOT can be asked to interpret text that follows "\".

Direct instructions in immediate mode are called *commands*; commands are obeyed when you press "RETURN".

Deferred instructions in a PILOT program are called *statements*; statements are obeyed when the program is run.

The command "LIST" will display the contents of the program space.

An alternation of T:, A:, T:, and so on will produce conversational interaction but with no recognition of the user's response.

M: allows recognition of one or more elements of the response.

The response (a string of characters) can be saved by designating a string variable name in the A: statement; for example, "A:$name".

When the string variable name appears in a T: statement, the string variable name is replaced by the stored response.

Responses can also be more permanently saved in a disk file.

PILOT SESSION QUIZ

```
list
T: This is a brief test of concepts in Chapter II.
T: It is of course written in PILOT.
T: Only PILOT functions already discussed will be used.
T:
T: When "READY" appears on the screen, it is
   likely that
T: you are in _____ mode.  (Type the fill-in word)
A:
M: immediate
TY: That's right.
T: You are probably in immediate mode.
T:
T: Press "RETURN" to go on.
```

```
A:
T: When you are in immediate mode, what should you type
T: if you wish to see a list of immediate commands?
A:
M: \?, question
TY: Yes.
T: You should type a question mark.
T:
T: Press "RETURN" to go on.
A:
T: In the run mode, PILOT tries to follow instructions that
T: have been stored in the program space. If there is nothing
T: there, what would you expect to see displayed?
A:
M: READY
TY: Yes, you would see just the word "READY".
TN: Since PILOT has nothing to interpret, it would return to
TN: immediate mode and display the word "READY".
T:
T: Press "RETURN" to go on.
A:
T:
T: If you see the message "*UNRECOGNIZED PILOT STATEMENT", it
T: means which of the following (Type 1, 2, or 3).
T:
T:     1. An immediate command is not one of those listed
T:        when you type "?".
T:     2. A line of text in the program space does not
T:        contain a colon.
T:     3. The text displayed above the message is not a legal
T:        PILOT statement.
A:
M: 1
TY:    You answered with a 1. That is incorrect.
TY: An unrecognized immediate command is simply ignored.
M: 2
TY:    You answered with a 2.
TY: That might be true, but a colon is just one requirement
TY: for a legal PILOT statement.
```

24

M: 3
TY: That's right.
T:
T: Text that cannot be interpreted as a legal PILOT statement
T: is displayed just above the message.
T:
T: Press "RETURN" to go on.
A:
T:
T: What are direct instructions in immediate mode called?
A:
M: commands
TY: Correct.
T: They are called commands.
T:
T: Instructions in a PILOT program are referred to as _____.
A:
M: statements
T:
TY: That's right.
T: They are called statements.
T:
T: Press "RETURN" to go on.
A:
T:
T: What is the command to display the contents of the program
T: space?
A:
M: list
TY: Right.
T: The command is "LIST".
T:
T: Press "RETURN" to go on.
A:
T:
T: If you write a PILOT statement like "A: $response" it means
T: that you wish to store the answer that a user gives to the
T: A: statement so that you can use it later in the program.
T: Is that a reasonable expectation? (True or False)

A:

M: T

TY: Yes, it might be used in a statement like:

TY: T: I know that you earlier said $response.

TN: You don't know that it will be used, but it can be

TN: retrieved if needed during the same program run.

T:

T: This is the end of a quiz for Chapter 2.

PILOT Core Statements

As you now know, a PILOT program consists of a sequence of PILOT statements that represent instructions to the computer. PILOT interprets each statement in turn and causes the computer to carry out the instruction each one represents. You have seen the operation of three types of statements: the T: (Type) statement, the A: (Accept) statement, and the M: (Match) statement. You have also seen how the M: statement can determine the effect of Y or N conditioners added to the T: statement. While a T: statement will always display whatever text follows the colon, a TY: or TN: statement may or may not display such text, depending on whether a preceding match was successful or not.

In this chapter, we will discuss the PILOT statements that are used in all versions of PILOT, for they form the core of the language. Some of these were briefly described as "the elements of conversation" in Chapter 1. Because they are so commonly and constantly used, they are abbreviated to just one letter. Like all PILOT statements, they are followed by a colon. Statements whose names are more than one letter are used to add additional useful features to PILOT, but they are not standardized for all versions. The core statements use the following letters: T, A, M, R, J, E, U, and C.

T: (TYPE)

The T: (Type) statement prompts the computer to display what you type after the colon. You have already seen many examples using the T: statement. The T: statement can be used to present information, ask a question, or prompt a response. It makes up one side of a conversation—the side that the computer represents in whatever role it is playing.

You have seen how TY: and TN: operate, in which the suffix "Y" causes the text to be displayed only if the last attempted match was successful; and "N" causes the reverse, only if the last attempted match was not successful. Because these functions are so frequent, PILOT allows Y: to be used for TY: and N: to be used for TN:.

Another convenience peculiar to the T: statement is the use of the colon alone when typing several T: statements sequentially. You may use T: on each line but if you wish, you may use just ":" to begin each line after the first line. The meaning of T: will be carried forward until another statement type occurs. The same is true for TY: (or Y:) and TN: (or N:), which means that the condition of display or no display that is determined by Y or N continues to be in effect for the continuation lines that begin with a colon.

Earlier examples have also demonstrated how previously stored information can be inserted in the display from a T: statement. When information is saved for later use, it is given a name that can be called upon for reference and retrieval. The storage location is called a *variable* because the contents referred to by the variable name can change. Sometimes, you may wish to store text information that consists of a string of characters; at other times, you may wish to store a numeric value that can be manipulated arithmetically. The stored information can either be a string of text characters or a numeric value, and the names that you must use to refer to them are different in form. String variable names begin with "$" and numeric variable names begin with "#". In the Nevada PILOT, string variable names can be as long as ten characters while numeric variable names are single letters. In the Apple PILOT and some related versions, string variable names are also terminated with "$"; for example, "$name$" instead of "$name".

The T: statement automatically *concatenates* (hooks together) elements of plain text, string variables, and numeric variables in whatever order they occur and displays the result. Although the T: statement can retrieve and compile information from these different sources, keep in mind that the end result is the display of text in a literal fashion. If you type "T:4+6", PILOT will display "4+6".

Normally, each T: statement causes the display to begin on

the next line—but this need not be so. A backward slash "\" at the end of a T: statement causes continuation on the same line. For example:

```
user  ->    list
PILOT ->    T:Print this \
  "         T:all \
  "         T:together.


user  ->    run
PILOT ->    Print this all together.
```

A TH: statement will also cause typing to "hang" at the end of the displayed text so it can accomplish the same result.

As you have seen in previous examples, an A: statement normally accepts (and echoes) a response at the beginning of a new line. The "\" symbol can be used to position the response location on the same line as a prompting question.

```
user  ->        list
PILOT ->        T:Please answer YES or NO. \
PILOT ->        A:


user->          run
PILOT/user ->   Please answer YES or NO. YES
```

A: (ACCEPT)

The A: (Accept) statement causes PILOT to wait for information, often an answer to a question, to be typed from the keyboard.

A: usually occurs on a line by itself. An alternation of T: and A: is sufficient to produce interaction between PILOT and its user, even if it is a very simple interaction without an ability to respond differently to different input. For example:

```
(What the user types will be shown in boldface to distinguish it
from what is typed by PILOT.)
list
T:If you type something back to me, I will tell you something
 :about the A: statement.
```

```
A:
T: The A: statement accepts one line of entry and puts it in
 : what is called the accept buffer. The M: statement makes
 : use of the accept buffer.
```

run

```
If you type something back to me, I will tell you something
about the A: statement.
```
OK, 'tell me about it.

```
The A: statement accepts one line of entry and puts it in
what is called the accept buffer. The M: statement makes
use of the accept buffer.
```

You can capture the entry and store it under a string variable name (prefixed by $) or, if it is numeric, you can store it under a numeric variable name (prefixed by #). In the following example, whatever the user types is stored in the string variable with the name "$whatever".

list

```
T: Type anything, and I will agree with it.
A: $whatever
T: I agree, $whatever
T: You will have to type a number for this one to work.
 : How many years have you gone to school?
A: #N
T: #N is quite a few years!
```

run

```
Type anything, and I will agree with it.
```
Computers are pretty dumb unless programmed.
```
I agree, Computers are pretty dumb unless programmed.
You will have to type a number for this one to work.
How many years have you gone to school?
```
11
```
11 is quite a few years!
```

You won't always want the computer to remember what has been typed but you will soon see a number of ways in which the ability to do so can be helpful.

M: (MATCH)

Once there is something in the accept buffer (usually an entry prompted by an A: statement), you can arrange for PILOT to see if some element of the entry matches something you expect will match. You can have PILOT look for one or more words or pieces of words, any one of which might match something that was typed. If PILOT finds a match, it sets a YES condition, and if it doesn't find a match, it sets a NO condition. Any PILOT statement can then be caused to be effective or ineffective by adding the letter Y or N to the statement name. You have already seen how this works with the T: statement; and it works the same way with *all* PILOT statements. In the following example, we make use of AY: and MY: to condition whether an A: and an M: statement will operate.

```
list
T: The M: statement looks for a _____ in an answer.
 : A fill-in question like this usually expects
 : just one correct entry.
 : What is a good answer in this case?
A:
M: match
TY: Right.
TN: I think you missed that.
T: I was thinking of "match".
 :
 : Are there times when you might want to count
 : various words as equally good?
A:
M: yes, sure, right, o. k.
TY: You have the idea.
TN: There are often synonyms you should consider.
T: This example has an M: statement with various
 : positive words.
 :
TY: Can an M: statement be written to match any word
 : beginning with a particular letter?
AY:
MY: y
```

```
TY: You would use a space followed by the letter.
T: This program has examples of some of these concepts.
```

Notice that the Y conditioner has been applied to A: and to M: statements as well as to T: statements. This means that if the preceding match was not successful (the one looking for "yes,sure,right,o.k."), then the question "Can an M: " will not be asked and the following A: and M: statements will not be active. The last question (about matching words beginning with a particular letter) will be asked only if the prior question about synonyms was judged correct. As soon as another M: statement has been processed, however, the effects of Y and N conditioners are based on whether the *latest* attempted match occurred or not. If the response to the question about synonyms is matched, then the next question will be asked. But as soon as the MY: statement is executed, the result of its attempted match is in control. If, on the other hand, the response to the question about synonyms is not matched, then all the following statements that contain the Y suffix will be ignored.

The following first shows the results of a run in which attempted matches are successful, and then a run in which matches are unsuccessful.

```
run
The M: statement looks for a _____ in an answer.
A fill-in question like this usually expects
just one correct entry.
What is a good answer in this case?
match
Right.
I was thinking of "match".

Are there times when you might want to count
various words as equally good?
I'm sure that's right
You have the idea.

This example has an M: statement with various
positive words.
```

Can an M: statement be written to match any word
beginning with a particular letter?
yes
You would use a space followed by the letter.
This program has examples of some of these concepts.

Now another run with different responses:

run
The M: statement looks for a _____ in an answer.
A fill-in question like this usually expects
just one correct entry.
What is a good answer in this case?
word
I think you missed that.
I was thinking of "match".

Are there times when you might want to count
various words as equally good?
Probably not
There are often synonyms you should consider.
This example has an M: statement with various
positive words.

This program has examples of some of these concepts.

As you can see in this program segment, the M: statement is a key
element in providing the computer with some recognition capacity. You obviously need such ability if you wish to develop a program with conversational interaction.

The M: statement makes it easy to consider more than one
possible match, for your program must try to be adaptable to the
many ways someone might respond to it. The burden is now on
you, the programmer, to think of those possible responses and to
phrase the text preceding the A: statement in a way that prompts
a recognizable response.

The list of possible matching items after the colon in an M:
statement is called the M-list and the separate elements are called
M-items. As stated in the program, spaces in an M-item can be an
important part of the attempted comparison. The following are

the formal rules that PILOT follows in scoring an M: statement to be "yes" or "no."

1. Each pattern in the M: statement has multiple blanks reduced to one.
2. The contents of the accept buffer has a blank added to each end and also has multiple blanks reduced to one.
3. A moving window scan of the response is made with each pattern until either a match is found or the input is exhausted. No distinction is made between upper- and lower-case letters.

In order to understand what a moving window scan is, imagine the M-item as a pattern painted on a window, which is then passed along in front of the text string in the accept buffer while looking for a match. The entire pattern on the window has to be duplicated somewhere in the text for a match to occur.

You can think of the accept buffer as a part of computer memory that is analogous to your own short-term memory. It is used over and over with each A: statement— any new information erases what was there before. If you foresee a need to make later use of an entry into the accept buffer, save it under a variable name. As shown earlier, this can be done by simply placing a variable name after the colon of the A: statement; for example, "A:$name".

If you wish to look for a possible match within an earlier entry that has been saved, you must put it into the accept buffer since M: works only with the contents of the accept buffer. A special form of the A: statement retrieves previously stored text into the accept buffer instead of accepting a keyboard entry. It looks like this: "A:=$name". You can recognize it by the equal sign after the colon, which means "Fill the accept buffer from the contents of $name rather than from the keyboard." Apple PILOT uses a special variable name for the accept buffer in order to achieve the same result.

R: (REMARK)

Can you imagine a statement that PILOT will completely ignore when the program is run but is nevertheless useful to have as part of the language? The R: statement will let you make a note about the program that may be helpful when you look at it later. You can give it a name, for example, what it tries to do, or add anything else you may want to say about it.

When you write a long or complicated program and then don't look at it for a while, you will be especially happy to find R: statements to remind you of what you had in mind when you wrote the program. You will see R: statements when you list the program, but a user of the program will not see them.

```
   list
R: This is an example of an R: statement.
R: It will appear only in a listing of the program.
R:
T: This program does nothing but display this line.

R: + + + + + + + + + + + + + + + + + + + + + + + + + + + + +
R: +                                                       +
R: +      YOU CAN MAKE LABELS FOR YOUR PROGRAMS        +
R: +                                                       +
R: + + + + + + + + + + + + + + + + + + + + + + + + + + + + +

   run
This program does nothing but display this line.
```

Some versions of PILOT also offer a way to allow remarks on the same line as another PILOT statement.

J: (JUMP)

PILOT statements are usually interpreted in sequence, one after another. But the J: statement lets you jump to another place in the program before you continue on. The J: statement knows where to go because you supply a *label* after the colon. The label is whatever name you choose to use as a marker for the destination of the jump: It can be recognized because it starts with an asterisk (*), so it looks like this: "*LABEL". The J: statement that takes you to the label looks like this: "J:LABEL" or "J:*LABEL". The leading "*" is optional as part of the J: statement but is required as part of the marker label.

Remember, the J: must always have a label name following it, and that label must appear as a *LABEL destination somewhere else in the program. The destination label can be on a line by itself or ahead of another PILOT statement separated by one or more spaces. It can be spotted by the asterisk.

The J: statement is often made conditional with "Y" or "N"; for example:

list
```
*START
   T: SHOULD I TYPE THIS AGAIN?
   A:
   M: YES
   JY: *START
   T: I'M THROUGH JUMPING FOR NOW.
```

Notice that the final T: statement will not be reached as long as "YES" is typed and the JY: statement causes a restart.

run
```
SHOULD I TYPE THIS AGAIN?
```
YES
```
SHOULD I TYPE THIS AGAIN?
```
YES
```
SHOULD I TYPE THIS AGAIN?
```
NO
```
I'M THROUGH JUMPING FOR NOW.
```

Use of the J: statement will help in avoiding multiple use of the Y: conditioner in an instance when your goal is to make the entire question sequence conditional. But don't rule out the use of the Y/N condition with the M: statement. If you wish to check for the occurrence of item one and item two in a response, then the following sequence is appropriate:

list
```
M: item1
MY: item2
JN: *nomatch
T: Both items found
```

In an earlier sample program, we used the Y/N switch to make one of the questions conditional, but it was a clumsy method. Here is how it looks if a J: statement were used instead.


```
list
T: The M: statement looks for a _____ in an answer.
 : A fill-in question like this usually expects
 : just one correct entry.
 : What is a good answer in this case?
A:
M: match
TY: Right.
TN: I think you missed that.
T: I was thinking of "match".
 :
 : Are there times when you might want to count
 : various words as equally good?
A:
M: yes, sure, right, o. k.
TY: You have the idea.
N: There are often synonyms you should consider.
T: This example has an M: statement with various
 : positive words.
 :
JN: *QUIT
T: Can an M: statement be written to match any word
 : beginning with a particular letter?
A:
M:  y
TY: You would use a space followed by the letter.
TN: If you use a space followed by the letter, then the
 : letter would have to be found at the beginning of a
 : word and not in the middle, after another letter.

*QUIT
T: This program has examples of some of these concepts.
```

First, a run with matching answers, as before:

run

The M: statement looks for a _____ in an answer.
A fill-in question like this usually expects
just one correct entry.
What is a good answer in this case?

match

Right.
I was thinking of "match".

Are there times when you might want to count
various words as equally good?

I'm sure that's right

You have the idea.
This example has an M: statement with various
positive words.

Can an M: statement be written to match any word
beginning with a particular letter?

yes

You would use a space followed by the letter.
This program has examples of some of these concepts.

And a run with no matches:

run

The M: statement looks for a _____ in an answer.
A fill-in question like this usually expects
just one correct entry.
What is a good answer in this case?

word

I think you missed that.

I was thinking of "match".
Are there times when you might want to count various words as
equally good?

Probably not

There are often synonyms you should consider.
This example has an M: statement with various

39

positive words.

This program has examples of some of these concepts.

Given the same responses, the program run is the same as before. However, you do not have to worry about the effect of one M: statement on the next, so the logic is somewhat simpler. The last question can now include an explanation using a TN: statement. I will leave it up to you to see why this was not possible with the first method in which we used AN: and MN:.

The J: statement is helpful here because the destination label is close at hand and can be easily seen. If the labels are more distant, the programming logic can become confusing—and there are better ways to keep the program readable. It is also a good idea to make the label names as meaningful as possible.

E: (END)

You can probably guess that the E: statement means the *end* of something. Although programs will end if there are no more statements for PILOT to interpret, at times you may want to end the program somewhere in the middle. The E: statement can, of course, be conditional, such as EY: or EN:, just as other statements.

The E: statement is also used to mark the end of a program module that is not a complete program in itself. You can create such a module, give it a name, and then use it by referring to the name. We'll discuss this more under the U: statement.

```
list
R: Control when you want to end the program.
R:
T: Do you want to read more about R: statements?
A:
M: yes
JY: REMARK
T: I guess we're finished then. Goodbye.
E:
*REMARK R: This section is about R: statements.
T: The R: statement lets you say something that might be
T: useful to a reader of the program.
```

```
T: That reader might be you at some time in the future.
T:
T: The program will now end.
E:
```

run
```
Do you want to read more about R: statements?
```
No
```
I guess we're finished then. Goodbye.
```

run
```
Do you want to read more about R: statements?
```
yes
```
The R: statement lets you say something that might be
useful to a reader of the program.
That reader might be you at some time in the future.
The program will now end.
```

In the first run of the program there was no match with the "yes" in the M: statement so the jump to *REMARK did not occur and the T: and E: statements were executed.

In the second run, the jump *did* occur and the program continued to display some additional T: statements.

U: (USE)

Like the J: statement, the U: statement interrupts the usual sequence of interpreting one PILOT statement after another. Also like the J: statement, U: requires that the name of a destination label be present after the colon. The U: statement, however, causes something else to happen in addition to the jump to a new place in the program. The U: statement causes PILOT to remember where it was when the jump occurred and to return to that spot when it reaches an E: statement that indicates the end of a program segment.

This means that you can create program segments, modules, or subroutines (these are similar) to perform a particular task. Just refer to them by name (for example, U:*name) and they will occur. The program module must begin with a *LABEL and end with an E: statement.

For those who have programmed in BASIC, the U: statement is similar to GOSUB, and the E: statement at the end of the module is similar to RETURN. Unlike BASIC, PILOT lets you use a meaningful name instead of a line number.

When you create a module that you will use via a U: statement, be careful to keep the module isolated from the main sequence of your program. The easiest way to do this is to place it after the E: statement that marks the end of your program, so that it takes an explicit U: statement reference to make it active.

Here is a program example:

```
list
T:Even a short program module can be helpful.
T:For instance, we might often want to accept an answer and
T:set the match condition on positive words.
T:Can you see how that is shown here?
U: *answer
Y:That's right. The subroutine looks for a match.
R: Remember how Y: and N: can be used for TY: and TN:
N:The U: statement causes *answer to be used. After
  :*answer waits for an answer (A:) and looks for a match
  :with any of the words in the M: statement, PILOT
  :returns and executes either TY: or TN:
  :Your answer did not match any of the words.
T:
T:Would it be OK to use *answer again?
U: *answer
Y:Good, you've got the idea.
N:There's no reason not to use it again.
T:It can be used as many times as we like.


E:
R: This E: statement is the end of our program.
R:Without E: here, we would "fall into" *answer and with
R:no question having been asked, our user wouldn't know
R:why PILOT was waiting for an answer.
R:If the user pressed RETURN, the E: would be interpreted
R:as the end of the program, since there would be no
R:return left to be used.
```

```
*answer
  A:
  M: yes,ok,sure,right
  E:
R: This E: statement is the end of the module named *answer.
```

run
```
Even a short program module can be helpful.
For instance, we might often want to accept an answer and
set the match condition on positive words.
Can you see how that is shown here?
```
Yes, I can
```
That's right. The subroutine looks for a match.

Would it be OK to use *answer again?
```
Yes, I think it would.
```
Good, you've got the idea.
It can be used as many times as we like.
```

Here we have used the subroutine to check for a number of words that might mean an affirmative response. Note the spaces that surround the word "yes." They may not be necessary here, but the spaces would avoid a match with such words as "keyes" or "yesterday." Spaces are significant in M: statements.

C: (COMPUTE)

Yes, PILOT can do arithmetic! Use the C: statement and numeric variables. Following the colon of the C: statement, PILOT expects to find first a variable, then an equal sign, and then an expression. The expression on the right side is evaluated to produce a value that is then assigned to the variable on the left side. That sounds complicated, but an easy numeric example will make it clear. If we write:

C: #A=4+3

the "4+3" is an expression that is evaluated to the value 7 and is assigned to the numeric variable A. This all happens internally within PILOT, since C: statements by themselves don't result in output that you can see. However, if you display the value of A, for example, "T: #A", you will see a new result.

Within a C: statement, the initial "#" of a numeric variable name is optional (although "#" is required in some PILOT systems). The C: statement example can be written as "C:A=4+3". From now on, the notation will be simplified in this way: The "#" is always required when a numeric variable is referred to in a T: or A: statement.

The expression on the right can also consist of variables; for example:

```
C:  A=7
C:  B=A+3
T:  A= #A,  B= #B
```

In the first line, #A is assigned the value of 7. In the second line, #B is assigned the value of #A+3, or 10. The third line will display

```
A =  7,  B =  10
```

Note that the equal sign is not used to indicate equivalence but rather to assign a new value to the variable on the left of the equal sign. (This convention is used in a number of other programming languages.) When the same variable appears on both sides of the equal sign, think of the right side as the old value and the left side as the new value. Thus, "N = N+1" will increase the value of N by 1, since it adds 1 to whatever is the old value of N and assigns the result to the new value of N. Now let's look at a more complex example:

```
list
R: This program will add numbers until the user enters 0.
T:Entered numbers will be added until 0 is entered.
C: S=0
*more T:Next number  \
  A: A
  M:  0
  JY: *sum
```

```
C: S=S+A
J: *more
*sum
T: The sum is #S
```

Before accepting input, the program sets an initial value of #S to zero. (You would not want #S to start with an unknown value since it is used as an accumulator of the sum.) Whenever a leading zero is entered (note the space in the M: statement), a match causes a jump to the final T: statement and the sum is displayed. Any other number is added to the current value of #S and a jump back to *more prompts for the entry of another number. A run of the program might look like this:

```
run
Entered numbers will be added until 0 is entered.
Next number 15
Next number 12
Next number 8
Next number 121
Next number 0
The sum is 156
```

The arithmetic operators in PILOT are + (add), − (subtract), * (multiply), / (divide), and % (return the remainder of a division). It would be easy to use the divide operator to have the last example display the average of entered numbers. You would need to use another numeric variable, such as #N, to be incremented every time there was a new entry. You would then have a value available for a C: statement such as:

```
C: A=S/N
```

in which the average could be produced from the values of the sum and the number of items.

```
list
T: This program will find the average of entered numbers.
T: Enter "9999" to stop entering numbers.
```

```
   C: S=0
   C: N=0
 *more T: Next number \
   A: A
   M:  9999 ,
   JY: *average
   C: S=S+A
   C: N=N+1
   J: *more
 *average
   C: A=S/N
   T: The average of #N entries is #A.
```

A frequent application of the C: statement within a PILOT instructional program would be to add up the scores resulting from responses to individual questions in a lesson and divide by the number of questions answered. This number might vary in a program that allowed different branching for different users.

In addition to the assignment of numbers, the C: statement can also evaluate a *text expression* and assign the result to a string variable. A string variable is indicated by an initial "$", just as in a T: or A: statement. The text expression on the right of the equal sign can have the same characteristics as the body of a T: statement: It can consist of any combination of text, string variable names, or numeric variable names. Replacement of values in place of names should occur, as in the T: statement. The result of such replacement will then be assigned to the string variable on the left of the equal sign. For example, if $name refers to "Tom" and #X contains the value "15", then the following C: statement would create a sentence and store it in the string variable $WORDS:

```
C: $WORDS=My name is $name and I am #X years old.
```

The sentence would read "My name is Tom and I am 15 years old." and it could be displayed by "T:$WORDS".

Some PILOTs, Apple PILOT, for example, do not follow this definition in all respects and require the addition of quotation marks to surround text on the right of the equal sign.

MAKING PILOT STATEMENTS CONDITIONAL

We have seen how the M: statement sets a *conditioner* of "Y" or "N" that may be used as a suffix to any instruction.

This makes the M: statement's operation conditional upon the result of the attempted match. Another conditioner of PILOT statements can be created by testing the relation between two numeric expressions. Relational operators are < (less than), > (greater than), = (equal), and <> (not equal). To make the operation of a PILOT statement conditional, the *relational expression* is placed within parentheses between the statement name and the required colon.

This may at first glance seem formidable, but without the big words, it's a simple and useful idea. You may have arranged for your program to count how many correct answers students obtain in a test. Every time a student chooses a correct answer, you have added to the value of numeric variable G with a C: statement (C:G=G+1). If a student gets more than twenty answers correct, you may wish to congratulate him. A relational expression "G>20" becomes true if the value G becomes larger than 20. You can therefore use a conditional T: statement like this:

```
T(G>20):CONGRATULATIONS !
```

Here are some other examples:

```
T(X > Y): This text will display if X is greater than Y.
T(A = B): This text will display if A is equal to B.
```

If the expression is evaluated as "true," the statement will be executed. A numeric value by itself is considered "true" if it is greater than zero.

```
T( N ): This will display if N is greater than zero.
```

SUMMARY

PILOT core statements are used in all versions of PILOT and are abbreviated to a single letter. They are:

　　T: (Type)

A: (Accept)

M: (Match)

R: (Remark)

J: (Jump)

E: (End)

U: (Use)

C: (Compute)

The T: (Type) statement will display whatever is typed following the colon. String variable names, beginning with "$", and numeric variable names, beginning with "#", cause values referred to by those names to be inserted in the text. Y: can be used as an abbreviation for TY: and N: can be used for TN:. A colon alone can be used for continuation lines.

The A: (Accept) statement will accept entry from the keyboard. The entry can be stored under a string variable name or, if it is numeric, under a numeric variable name. In any case, the entry is kept in the accept buffer where it can be used by the M: statement. A statement such as "A:$NAME" will retrieve what is stored in $NAME and place it in the accept buffer.

The M: (Match) statement attempts to match each of the items listed after the colon with the contents of the accept buffer. A match of any item causes a "YES" condition to be set; if no item matches, a "NO" condition is set. Statements ending in "Y" are obeyed only if the "YES" condition is set; and statements ending in "N" are obeyed only if the "NO" condition is set.

The R: (Remark) statement has no effect on program operation but allows you to say something about the program.

The J: (Jump) statement always has a label name following the colon and the name matches a label somewhere in the program. The label to be matched looks like "*LABEL" and is at the beginning of a line, either by itself or separated by one or more blanks from a PILOT statement.

The E: (End) statement marks the end of a PILOT program or the end of a program module, also called a subroutine.

The U: (Use) statement causes a jump to the label named after the colon and also a return to the immediately following statement when E: is encountered.

The C: (Compute) statement allows assignment statements to be written for either numeric or string variables. The statement

must have an equal sign. An expression to the right is evaluated
and the resulting value is assigned to a variable on the left.

PILOT SESSION QUIZ

```
list
T: This is a test of some of the concepts in Chapter 3.
T: It is written in PILOT.
T: Only PILOT functions already discussed will be used.
     R: I will keep track of the number correct in variable c
     R: and the number of questions in variable n.
     C: c=0
     C: n=0
T: At any time you may give an immediate command to jump to
T:     another question or to the end by typing "\J:*Qn"
T:     (n= question no.) or "\J:END" and two carriage returns.
T: For example, if you wish to jump to question 5 you should type
T:     "\J:Q5" and then press RETURN twice.

*Q1    R: I will use a label on each question for possible
          R: reference.
T:
T: What is one of the characteristics of PILOT core statements
T: that are used in all versions of the language?
A:
     C: n=n+1
R:        Any one of the following will turn on the "Y" switch.
M: single,one,colon
Y: Yes, they are abbreviated to one letter followed by a colon.
     CY: c=c+1
N: These are the most commonly used statements. They are
N:     abbreviated to one letter.
T:
T: Press "RETURN" to go on
A:
*Q2
T: The PILOT statement that will display whatever is typed after
```

```
T:    the colon is the _____ statement. Enter a single letter.
A:
     C: n=n+1
M:  T ,
R:    The comma in the M: statement causes a space to be required
R:       after T.
Y: Right.
     CY: c=c+1
N: You should think of the T: statement.
T:
T: Press "RETURN" to go on
A:
*Q3
T: An A: statement can accept an answer and also store it as a
T:    string variable. A T: statement can make use of the stored
T:    answer.
T:
T: Consider the sequence:
T:       T: What name would you like me to call you?
T:       A: $title
T:
T: How would you write a T: statement later on in the same program
T:    in order to say goodbye to the user by name?
T:    Choose a number.
T:
T:       (1)   T: Goodbye, $title.
T:       (2)   T: Goodbye, user.
T:       (3)   T: Goodbye, $name.
T:       (4)   T: Goodbye, title.

*Q3more
A:
     C: n=n+1
M:  1 ,
Y: Yes, "$title" will be replaced by whatever name was entered.
     CY: c=c+1
JY: *Q3end
M:  2 , 3 , 4 ,
```

50

Y: No, the user's name is stored under the variable name "$title".
N: You must answer with 1, 2, 3, or 4.
JN: *Q3more

*Q3end
T:
T: Press "RETURN" to go on
A:

*Q4
T: The M: statement looks for a _____ with an element of the last
T: answer.
T: Type the missing word.
A: $answer4
     C: n=n+1
M: match
T: You answered "$answer4".
Y: That's what I was hoping you would type.
     CY: c=c+1
N: But I was hoping you would type "match".
T:
T: Press "RETURN" to go on
A:

*Q5
T: Which statement has NO effect on how the program operates?
A:
     C: n=n+1
M: R: , R-, R , remark
Y: Right.
     CY: c=c+1
T: The R (remark) statement doesn't change program operation.
T: It lets the program author make comments about the program.
T:
T: Press "RETURN" to go on
A:

```
*Q6
T: A J:  statement MUST have something after the colon.  (T or F)
A:
    C: n=n+1
M:  T , true,  Y , yes
    R: I'll also allow Y for yes
Y: Yes.
     CY: c=c+1
T: It must have the name of a label that marks another place in
T:      the program.
T:
T: Press "RETURN" to go on
A:

*Q7
T: The U:  statement lets you use a program segment
T:
T:          (1)  just once.
T:          (2)  a preset number of times.
T:          (3)  as many times as you like.


*Q7more
A:
    C: n=n+1
M:  3 ,
Y: Correct, you can use it over and over.
     CY: c=c+1
JY: *Q7end
M:  1 ,  2 ,
Y: You can use it many times if you wish.
N: You must answer with 1, 2, or 3.
JN: *Q7more


*Q7end
T:
T: Press "RETURN" to go on
A:
```

*Q8

T: An E: statement marks the end of a _____.

T: More than one word is correct. Type one of them.

A:

       C: n=n+1

M: program, subroutine, module, segment.

Y: Yes.

       CY: c=c+1

T: The E: statement marks the end of a program module

T: (subroutine, segment) or the end of the entire program.

T:

T: Press "RETURN" to go on

A:

*Q9

T: What symbol must always be present in a C: statement?

A:

       C: n=n+1

M: = , equal

Y: That's right.

       CY: c=c+1

N: There must always be an equal sign.

T:

T: Press "RETURN" to go on

A:

*Q10

T: The C: statement evaluates an expression on the RIGHT or LEFT

T: side?

A:

       C: n=n+1

M: right

Y: Yes.

       CY: c=c+1

T: The result of evaluating what is on the right side of the equal

T: sign is then stored in the variable on the left side.

T:

53

*END

T: Press "RETURN" to see your score.
A:
T: You answered #c correctly out of #n questions.
E:

Helpful Additions

The core statements make up the necessary basics of the PILOT language. Since they provide the elements of conversational interaction, we can manage to program a great deal by using just these few statement types. There is another advantage to doing this: The program will then be more likely to run without modification on many different PILOT systems.

Here we will discuss a few common additions to PILOT. Some of these add new features while others just make things a little easier for the program author, providing a shortcut to the programming effort. Keep in mind that these and other additions may not exist in this form in all versions of PILOT. Appendix II offers information about some of the differences.

CURSOR AND VIDEO CONTROL

Although PILOT can operate with a printing terminal or teletype, most computers now provide the user with a video display terminal. A PILOT program can benefit from an ability to control the display.

A mark called the *cursor* indicates the current position on the display, the position where the next character will appear if typed. Think of the cursor as having an address in terms of its position by row and column. PILOT lets us set the cursor address and therefore control where the next display will occur.

CA: (Cursor address) CA: sets the cursor by row and column. For example, CA:5,10 causes the cursor to move to row 5 and column 10. If the next statement is a T:, that is where the text will begin; if the next statement is an A:, then that is where the input will be displayed as it is accepted.

CH: (Clear and home) This statement clears the screen and sets the cursor address to the home position of row one and column one. It is often used to separate questions or topics by presenting a new screen image rather than adding new text at the bottom of the screen, which will cause the screen to scroll.

CL: (Clear to end of line) This statement clears from the current cursor position to the end of the current line and does not change the cursor address.

CE: (Clear to end of screen) This statement clears from the current cursor position to the end of the last line on the screen and does not change the cursor address.

VARIOUS AIDS TO CONVERSATION

FOOT: (Foot of Screen Halt and Prompt)

You may have noticed some repetition in looking at the coding of the quiz at the end of Chapter 3. In order to pause and allow comments to be read before going on to the next question, there is a sequence like this:

```
T:
T:Press "RETURN" to go on
A:
```

Some PILOTs have a helpful statement "FOOT:" which allows a pause, placing the prompting line at the bottom of the screen. If text is supplied after the colon, then that text is displayed instead of the standard text:

PA: (Pause)

Sometimes it would be convenient to display something for the PILOT user to see but not require a response before going on to display something else. The PA: statement halts program operation for a specified length of time, indicated by a number or a numeric variable after the colon. The unit value of the number may differ in different PILOT systems. The most common units are either seconds or tenths of a second.

Since the PA: statement lets you control the amount of time that a student has to study information presented with preceding T: statements, it is useful for a variety of timed exercises. An example would be a test of reading comprehension, with the presentation of a reading passage followed by questions about what the reader understood or remembered.

Sometimes PA: is useful when giving a brief status report to the user. For example:

```
T: You have successfully completed Part 2.
PA: 5
```

VNEW: (New Variables)

We have seen that certain PILOT statements collect information from the user and save it for later use. For example, the A: statement, in the form of A:$name, can collect the user's response and save it for later reference as a string variable. The A: statement can also save a numeric response that can be referenced as a numeric variable. The C: statement can also store information in either the string or numeric mode. Although most of the time there is no problem in using such storage freely, sometimes there is a need to erase this stored information and start over. That is what VNEW: allows you to do. If you use VNEW: (without anything after the colon), then string variables are erased (and the space in memory reclaimed) and numeric variables are reset to zero.

Using VNEW:$ will erase only string variables; VNEW:#

58

will zero the numeric variables without affecting the stored string information.

XI: (Execute Immediate)

Some versions of PILOT have a powerful (but sometimes confusing) kind of statement that causes PILOT to interpret the contents of a string variable that follows the colon as a PILOT statement. For example, if the statement is

```
XI: $GREETING
```

and the contents of $GREETING is "T:Hello there", then the result would be execution of the T: statement, resulting in the display of "Hello there". You might ask why you would want to do that. Well, perhaps your program was designed to create different greetings under different conditions. This would be one way to do it. You probably wouldn't use XI: if the text after the colon was always the same. The advantage occurs when there is reason to create changeable operation, perhaps as a result of information entered by the user. For example, your program might ask the user:

```
T: Which question did you want to review?
 : They are named Q1, Q2, etc.
A: $WHICH
C: $CHOICE = J: *$WHICH
XI: $CHOICE
```

In this case, if the user enters Q2, then the contents of $WHICH becomes "Q2" and the C: statement causes $CHOICE to have the contents "J:*Q2". This is the statement that is executed. Be careful to think through the sequence of operation so that the text in the XI: statement will, in fact, be a valid PILOT statement and will be one that is intended. When creating a program segment of this type, it is often useful to insert a temporary T: statement (in this case, "T:$CHOICE") just ahead of the XI: statement. Try some test entries and then remove the T: statement when everything is working properly.

CALL: (Call Existing Program)

It is sometimes helpful to be able to couple a PILOT program to an existing program written in another programming language. PILOT makes it especially easy to write interactive "front ends" for other systems, perhaps asking users which of several programs they would like to run. After the information is obtained, PILOT ought to be able to start the other program and perhaps send it some useful data. There are two ways to do this, depending on whether the external program is already in the computer's memory or exists as an executable file on external storage such as a disk.

The CALL: statement takes care of the case when a program, separate from PILOT, already exists in memory. You must know the memory address where the separate program begins, and indicate this address after the colon. You can also make available a numeric value that can be used by the other program. You need to know very specific things about the operation of your particular computer in order to use the CALL: statement, so this won't be discussed further.

XS: (Execute from the System)

An alternative way to initiate operation of another program is to drop out of PILOT and give a command to the operating system. This is the system (such as CP/M) that will accept a command to execute a program from a disk file. Rather than asking the user to exit PILOT and enter the system command, the XS: statement allows you, the PILOT programmer, to write a command into the PILOT program. The system command, for whatever operating system PILOT is running under, is given after the colon in the XS: statement. For example, your PILOT program may have created a data file that you wish to analyze with a BASIC program. After creating the data file, the PILOT program could use the XS: statement:

```
XS:BASIC ANALYSIS
```

which would cause loading of the BASIC system and operation of a BASIC program called ANALYSIS.

SUMMARY

Some common additions to PILOT are the following:

Cursor and screen controls

CA: Cursor address to set row and column
CH: Clear and home
CL: Clear to end of line
CE: Clear to end of screen

Various other aids to conversation

FOOT: Foot of screen halt and prompt
PA: Pause
VNEW: New variables
XI: Execute immediate
CALL: Call existing program
XS: Execute from the System

The FOOT: statement places a prompting line at the bottom of the screen and waits for a response before proceeding.

The PAUSE: statement halts program operation for a specified length of time and then continues.

The VNEW: statement erases string or numeric variables.

The XI: statement obeys the contents of a string variable, which should be a valid PILOT statement.

The CALL: statement provides a way to call upon the operation of a program that exists in the computer memory external to PILOT.

The XS: statement calls upon the computer operating system to initiate operation of another program.

PILOT SESSION QUIZ

```
R: CHAPTER 4 QUIZ
CH:
T: These are some questions about the ideas in Chapter 4,
T: written in PILOT.
    R: I will keep track of the number correct in variable c
    R: and the number of questions in variable n.
    C: c=0
```

```
    C: n=0
T: At any time, you may give an immediate command to jump to
:      another question or to the end by typing "\J:Qn"
:      (n= question no.) or "\END:" and two returns.


*Q1
T:
T: If you write "CA:5,12" on the line before a T statement, the
T: text that gets displayed will start on what line? :\
     c: n=n+1
A:
M: 5 , five
TY: and in what column? \
A:
MY: 12 , twelve
    cy: c=c+1
TY: That's right.
T: The next display will start on line 5 and column 12.
FOOT:


*Q2 CH:
T:
T: Cursor addressing can be useful for fill-in questions.
T: It can cause an answer to be entered in just the right c_____.
CA: 3,57
A:
    c: n=n+1
M: olumn
    cy: c=c+1
T:
T: Here you see one way that it can look.
FOOT:


*Q3 CH:
T:
T: If you write "FOOT: Study the above, then press RETURN", you
:    expect everything after the colon to appear on the
:    _____ line of the screen. Type the missing word.
```

A:
   C: n=n+1
M: bottom, last, final
Y: Yes.
   CY: c=c+1
N: No.
T: The text is displayed on the bottom line of the screen.
FOOT:

*Q4 CH:
T:
T: During the pause initiated by a PA: statement, can a user
T: enter information through the keyboard? (Y or N)
A:
   C: n=n+1
M: N
Y: Right.
   CY: c=c+1
N: No.
T: The keyboard will not accept entry during the pause.
T: We are now pausing for a few seconds, so you can try it.
PA: 20
T:
T:

*Q5 CH:
T:
T: You probably won't have much occasion to use VNEW: $ unless
 : you save a lot of text in string variables and run out of
 : memory space.
   R: The back slash below avoids the normal substitution
   R: of a numerical value in a T: statement.
T: VNEW: \#, though, might be useful before asking a new
 : numerical test question. Would it hurt anything to use it
 : in the middle of this sequence of questions? (Y or N)
A:
   C: n=n+1
   R: Note that M: checks for the WRONG answer.

R: See what that does to the logic.

M: N

Y:Well, we would lose our count of questions and how many
 :were correct.

    CN: c=c+1

N: If you said YES you were on the right track, since VNEW: \#
 :would lose our count of questions and the number correct.

FOOT:

*Q6 CH:

T:

T:Assume that the variable $SAYIT has the contents:

T: A: $NAME

T:

T:Would the following be a legal PILOT statement?

T: XI: $SAYIT

A:

   C: n=n+1

M: Y,

Y:Yes, it would cause the user's entry to be stored in
 :the variable $NAME.

    CY: c=c+1

N:The XI: statement would cause the contents of $SAVIT
 :to be retrieved and executed as a PILOT statement.
 :Since "A: $NAME" is a legal PILOT statement, it would
 :go ahead to store the user's entry in $NAME.

FOOT:

*Q7 CH:

T:

T: If you wish to leave PILOT and execute another program
 :as though you were giving a command to the computer's
 :operating system, what is the PILOT statement that
 :will let you do it?

A:

   C: n=n+1

M: XS

Y: That's right

    CY: c=c+1

T: The XS: statement will exit PILOT and send information
 : to the operating system.

*END
T: Press "RETURN" to see your score.
A:
T: You answered #c correctly out of #n questions.
 :

Developing Programs

OUTLINING PROGRAM GOALS

If you have an overall idea for a program, it is often helpful to jot down your first thoughts about sequence without regard to the details of PILOT coding. Then try to identify the major elements of operation and assign them names. The names can later become the labels for program modules or subroutines.

In developing a test with instructional elements, for example, you might make some notes, just using whatever words come to mind. This is similar to what you would write if you were giving directions to another person to carry out the operations. Here is a sample of such an informal draft for a program describing computer terminology.

Introduce the topic of computer terms.
Tell the purpose of the program.
Show some terms.
Let the user choose one term.
Let the user quit upon request.
Ask a question about the chosen term.
Get an answer and score it.
Show a definition if the user wants it.
Let the user choose another term.
Repeat as before.

Defining Desired Inputs and Outputs

In writing your first informal notes about what you want the program to do, it is often helpful to sketch the appearance of the screen that you would like the user to see. The way a question is presented has a lot to do with how it may be answered, and you will need to make some guesses about user responses in order to properly recognize the answers.

But first consider the more general organization of what is proposed. Let's turn some elements of the outline into PILOT coding but without concern for minor details. T: statements can be used as temporary indicators of something not yet made operational.

```
list
*intro
T: Computers are becoming so commonplace that almost everyone
 : needs to be familiar with computer terms, particularly those
 : relating to small computers. This will be a quiz about some
 : of them.

*terms
T:
T: <<< Show some terms here >>>
T:
T: Choose one of the above or type "quit".
A: $choice
M: quit
JY: quit
T:
T: <<< Check for term and go to proper question/definition >>>
T:
J: terms

*quit E:
```

Although the program is incomplete, with some of the contents missing, it is a perfectly legal PILOT program and can be run in order to test the overall logic. The T: statements that indicate incomplete sections act as "stubs" to be replaced later with more detail. It is often helpful to use some obvious marking to indicate the incomplete status of certain sections. Here is the incomplete program so far in operation.

The incomplete sections are shown by "<<< what is missing >>>".

run

    Computers are becoming so commonplace that almost everyone
needs to be familiar with computer terms, particularly those
relating to small computers. This will be a quiz about some
of them.

<<< Show some terms here >>>
Choose one of the above or type "quit".
term

<<< Check for each term and go to proper question/definition >>>

<<< Show some terms here >>>

Choose one of the above or type "quit".
quit

    READY

For the next stage of development, the section "Show some terms
here" can be replaced by T: statements displaying the terms. For
example:

T: backup	boot	chip	compiler
T: bit	byte	command	cursor

Then an M: statement and a JY: statement must be supplied for
each term in order to reach a place in the program where an appropriate question is asked or a definition is supplied. You can
look for each word just as in recognizing "quit". The program
would look like the following, in which we have changed the temporary T: statements into R: statements, using them as commen-
tary when we filled in details of operation.

list
*intro
T: Computers are becoming so commonplace that almost everyone
 : needs to be familiar with computer terms, particularly those

```
 : relating to small computers. This will be a quiz about some
 : of them.


*terms
T:
R: <<< Show some terms here >>>
     T: backup      boot      chip        compiler
     T: bit         byte      command     cursor
T:
T: Choose one of the above or type "quit".
A: $choice
R: <<< Check for term and go to proper question/definition >>>
   M: quit
   JY: *quit
   M: backup
   JY: *backup
   M: bit
   JY: *bit
   M: boot
   JY: *boot
   M: byte
   JY: *byte
   M: chip
   JY: *chip
   M: command
   JY: *command
   M: compiler
   JY: *compiler
   M: cursor
   JY: *cursor
J: terms
*backup: T: <<< backup >>>
     J: terms
*bit T: <<< bit >>>
     J: terms
*boot T: <<< boot >>>
     J: terms
```

```
*byte T: <<< byte >>>
    J: terms
*chip T: <<< chip >>>
    J: terms
*command T: <<< command >>>
    J: terms
*compiler T: <<< compiler >>>
    J: terms
*cursor T: <<< cursor >>>
    J: terms
*quit T: Goodbye
    E:
```

JM: (JUMP ACCORDING TO MATCH)

Instead of a long sequence of M: and JY: statements, there is another statement type available in many versions of PILOT. The JM: statement allows a branching of program logic, depending on which item in the M list was matched.

In the present instance, the following two statements can replace eighteen statements (a sequence of ten pairs of M: followed by JY).

```
M: quit, backup, bit, boot, byte, chip, command, compiler, cursor
JM: quit, backup, bit, boot, byte, chip, command, compiler, cursor
```

The items listed in the JM: statement are label names that must be present as destinations elsewhere in the program. For example, there must be a line starting with "*quit"; that one already exists in our incomplete program. The names used in the item lists of the M: statement and the JM: statement do not need to be the same, but the order is very important. If the third item in the M: statement is matched, then the third label in the JM: statement becomes the destination, whatever its name. For example, the M: statement should use "quit", if that's what the user is expected to say, but the first item in the JM: statement might use another label name, such as "end."

If no items are matched, then no jump occurs and program operation proceeds to the next statement on the following line. If there were more terms presented in the display, then another M: statement might follow to allow selection of others.

The program can now be revised by using the T: statements to present some terms and adding the M: and JM: statements for recognition of the response. An easy way to retain meaningful comments about program operation is to simply change the descriptive stubs from T: statements to R: statements. Once the JM: statement is added, we must provide the matching labels in order to keep the program operational. The use of stubs will be helpful once again.

```
list
*intro
T: Computers are becoming so commonplace that almost everyone
 : needs to be familiar with computer terms, particularly those
 : relating to small computers. This will be a quiz about some
 : of them.

*terms
T:
R: <<< Show some terms here >>>
    T: backup     boot     chip        compiler
    T: bit        byte     command     cursor
T:
T: Choose one of the above or type "quit".
A: $choice
R: <<< Check for term and go to proper question/definition >>>
        M: quit,backup,bit,boot,byte,chip,command,compiler,cursor
        JM: quit,backup,bit,boot,byte,chip,command,compiler,cursor
J: terms

*backup: T: <<< backup >>>
        J: terms
*bit T: <<< bit >>>
        J: terms
*boot T: <<< boot >>>
        J: terms
*byte T: <<< byte >>>
        J: terms
```

72

```
*chip T: <<< chip >>>
      J: terms
*command T: <<< command >>>
      J: terms
*compiler T: <<< compiler >>>
      J: terms
*cursor T: <<< cursor >>>
      J: terms
*quit T:
      T: Goodbye
      E:
```

Once again, the incomplete program can be run to test its development. This time, actual terms can be chosen, and the stubs indicate where further content should be added.

run
```
Computers are becoming so commonplace that almost everyone
needs to be familiar with computer terms, particularly those
relating to small computers. This will be a quiz about some
of them.
backup     boot     chip      compiler
bit        byte     command   cursor

Choose one of the above or type "quit".
```
boot
```
 <<< boot >>>

backup     boot     chip      compiler
bit        byte     command   cursor

Choose one of the above or type "quit".
```
cursor
```
<<< cursor >>>

backup     boot     chip      compiler
bit        byte     command   cursor
```

```
Choose one of the above or type "quit".
quit

Goodbye
READY
```

With the basic structure in place, it is easy to see how you can complete the details of the program. You can, for example, replace the line *cursor T: <<< cursor >>> with the following section to ask about "cursor" and provide a definition if requested.

```
list
*cursor R:  <<< cursor >>>
 CH:
 T: The main purpose of the cursor is to show a _____ on
  : the display screen.
 CA: 1, 45
 A:
 M: location, position, place, spot
 Y: That's a good answer.
 N: I'm not sure you have the idea.
 T: Would you like to see a definition?
 A:
 M:  y
 JN: terms

 T: A cursor is the rectangle or underline, perhaps
  : blinking, that is visible on the video display screen.
  : It shows the screen position at which the next
  : character will be displayed.
 J: terms
```

It might be a good idea to test a section like this separately before inserting it into the main program, since it is easier to edit and refine this portion without having to go through the preliminaries of running the rest of the program.

```
run
The main purpose of the cursor is to show a location on
the display screen.
```

That's a good answer.
Would you like to see a definition?
yes
A cursor is the rectangle or underline, perhaps
blinking, that is visible on the video display screen.
It shows the screen position at which the next
character will be displayed.
*TERMS -NOT FOUND
Press "RETURN" to go on

READY

In the actual execution of the program, the cursor was positioned
at the beginning of the fill-in area, so the word "location" was
typed in the proper place. The display of "*TERMS -NOT
FOUND" was not a part of the program we wrote but is caused by
the PILOT interpreter complaining that it cannot find the label
"*TERMS" that is referenced in the last line of our program segment by the final J: statement. Although it is in our main program, it is not present when we run this section separately.

THE USE OF SUBROUTINE MODULES
FOR LOGICAL DESIGN

If you find that the same operation is to be carried out at several
places in the program, there is an alternative to repeating the
same instructions in each place. One copy of the instructions can
be packaged as a "module" or "subroutine" by placing a label at
the beginning of the module and an E: statement at the end.
Then this package can be called into play by means of the U: statement. Think of the "U" as "use" of the module. After the module
performs its task and the E: statement is reached, then the program continues on with the statement that follows the U:
statement.
    The module does a number of useful things. Obviously, it
saves memory space when compared to repetition of the same sequence of instructions, but it also makes it easier to visualize the
organization of a program, especially if the program becomes
large or complex. If modules are assigned meaningful names

along with descriptive comments about specifically what they do, they can be an element in a library of useful components for other programs. When you create a module in PILOT, think of it as an extension of the PILOT language, thus adding a personal tool to those provided in the standard set.

As a simple example, you might find yourself repeatedly needing a function to check for various forms of agreement that might be given in response to a question such as "Do you agree?" An example of a brief module follows:

```
list
*checkyes
    R:Accept input and save in $yes
    R:Return with the result of an attempted match for various
    R:   yes words.
A: $yes
N: yes,sure,right,aye,ok,agree
E:
```

Whenever your program asks a question and accepts an answer of this kind, insert "U:checkyes" and follow on with appropriate use of "Y" and "N" conditioners as a result of the M: statement contained in the module. The portion of a program that would call upon use of this module might look something like the following:

```
. . .
T:  Do you agree?
U:  *checkyes
TY: Good, I'm glad you agree.
JY: *agree
JN: *noagree

. . .
```

After returning from *checkyes, the "Y" and "N" conditioners will operate according to whether or not any of the "yes" words were matched. Furthermore, if you found in the course of usage of your program that another synonym was necessary in the M: statement, then it would only be necessary to add it in this one place rather than in the many places where you might have otherwise written a similar sequence.

The R: statements are probably not necessary for this short and simple module, but it is a good habit to explain what a module does; this will reap rewards when the operation is more complex.

Modules may use other modules in a nested fashion, to a depth of eight in most PILOT systems: Eight modules is a generous limit for most PILOT applications. PILOT does not allow a module to call on itself or on another module that calls on itself. That is, if module A uses module B, then B cannot in turn make use of A—nor can it "recursively" make use of B.

THE USE OF OVERLAYS
AND LARGE PROGRAM SEGMENTS

In most PILOT-systems operations on small computers, the program to be run is entirely loaded into computer memory before the program starts to operate. The memory may not be sufficient to contain everything you wish to include; you need to consider how best to deal with the program material in sections. If the overall structure of the program is linear so that you expect the user to progress from part one to part two, and so on, then your problem is relatively simple. At the end of section one your program will issue a command to load the next section; for example, "LOAD: SECT2". Unless you instruct otherwise, both numeric and string variables developed in section one will remain available to the operation. If section one contains general-purpose modules, such as the *checkyes module just described, then a copy of that needs to be included in section two. Section two can, of course, load a further section or reload section one.

Perhaps there are choices to be made about the sequence of sections, and different users may not experience them in the same order. In keeping with the design philosophy presented in this chapter, it is often useful to consider the first section of a large program as a kind of master control, setting out a menu of options from which to choose. If you know that the choices are of considerable size, then each will require the loading of a new section. Here is an example:

```
list
    R: ++++++ LESSONS ++++++
    R: This section provides a menu of lesson choices.
```

```
R:A choice results in loading a lesson,  then reloading this.
*lessons
CH:
CA: 8
T: There are eight lessons,  each describing the use of one of the
T: PILOT core statements.
CA: 14
T:           T: (Type)       J:  (Jump)
T:           A: (Accept)     E:  (End)
T:           M: (Match)      U:  (Use)
T:           R: (Remark)     C:  (Compute)
T:
T:
FOOT: Choose one of the above or "Q" to quit --->
CA: 24, 54
M:  t
TY: loady: tlesson
M:  a
TY: loady: alesson
M:  m
TY: loady: mlesson
M:  r
TY: loady: rlesson
M:  j
TY: loady; jlesson
M:  e
TY: loady: elesson
M:  u
TYloady: ulesson
M:  c
TY: loady: clesson
M:  q
EY:
PA: 5
J: lessons
```

This sample program uses the CA: statement to place information
in specific locations on the display screen. It also uses the FOOT:

statement to prompt a response, replacing the standard text element of FOOT: with one appropriate for this use. The M: statements are written with a leading space so that they will match either a single letter, the letter plus a colon, or a word beginning with the letter. When the program is fully operational, each M: statement will be followed by a statement; for example, "loady:tlesson". These cannot be used, however, until program files such as "tlesson" or "tlesson.plt" exist. Until then, you can make them inoperative by preceding them with R: or make them visible by preceding them with TY:. In this case, using T: will let you see what is supposed to happen when you run the incomplete program. As soon as there are labeled program files available, the leading TY: can be removed and the desired statement will be enabled.

Temporary display of the disabled instruction will not work well until two other elements (also temporary) are added. The statement "ca:24,54" causes the display (whichever TY: statement is activated) to be located a few spaces after the user's response (prompted by FOOT:). The "pa:5" statement gives the viewer a chance to see the selected display before the screen is rewritten with a new set of choices. These two statements can be removed when the program files are available to be loaded. Each of the sub-programs must, of course, end with the reloading of the original master program with a statement such as "load:lessons" so that control returns to the first and major program section for further choice.

DEVELOPING PROGRAMS
WITH FLEXIBILITY FOR CHANGE

In developing a complex program, it is helpful to keep in mind a hierarchy of elements, increasing in size from individual PILOT statements to brief modules that act as extensions to the standard statement types to larger modules that act as logical sections of the overall program. Then, if necessary, larger program sections can be developed; they must be loaded from a secondary storage device.

It is not necessary to have these levels defined before starting to create a program in draft form. When you develop a rough sketch of the program, use T: statements to indicate what is expected to be accomplished by each section. As you come across an operation that seems likely to be needed in another place, you can define it as a module. Again, use a T: statement to indicate what the module function is and continue writing the main program. When you have finished sketching the main program, take up each of the modules (the major ones first), making note of sub-modules as you go.

During this process, your first ideas about major structure and what modules will be useful may change. Rewrite the T: statements to reflect this before moving onto detailed coding. The detail will reflect matters of appearance on the screen and the choice of specific elements to recognize within responses from the user. These are better left to a later stage.

EFFECTIVE PRESENTATION OF INFORMATION

In addition to developing the logic of your PILOT program, you must be concerned with its ability to communicate. Far from being merely a cosmetic detail, the effective use of the video screen for presenting information and prompting useful responses deserves some thought and planning. I assume that you would like your program to appear friendly and helpful to its user. This not only requires that you be clear about the aims of your program but also requires that you know something about the characteristics of your users and the setting in which the program will operate.

As a basic guideline, avoid confusing your user by keeping your instructions direct and your programs simple. PILOT allows for many clever effects, some of which will tempt you into making a complex interaction with the user. But the user should not be left wondering what is happening and how the program works.

There is no need to fill the display screen just because there are lots of character positions available. The dialog with your user may move along more smoothly with a simple display that presents information in digestible portions.

You can help the user to stay alert to your program's status by providing a heading or title on the screen. If the program uses a menu or list of options from which to begin a new section, the title on the new section can duplicate the option chosen. Users will appreciate such easy perception of the program's logic, and it will make the sequence apparent.

Some programs can be organized as a sequence of successive images or displays. For these, a technique called a *storyboard*, used for the development of television scripts, can be helpful. Stores that carry supplies for graphic artists have layout pads that feature multiple segments on each page in the shape of a television screen. You can use these pads as a guide during your initial design to help you visualize the sequence of what the user of your program will see.

ADAPTING TO THE SKILL
OF THE PROGRAM USER

In an application such as repeated data entry, users become increasingly skilled and require much less prompting or continued direction. If your application is one in which you anticipate repeated use and increasing skill, consider a means for your program to identify advanced users and adapt to their needs. Prompts and reminders need not be as extensive, and abbreviated responses can be allowed. For example, you can provide "shortcuts" through the sequence of your program by the use of conditional instructions. Such instructions would skip past unnecessary explanations that an advanced user no longer needs.

Timing is also an important consideration. Users have expectations based on how most people will respond to a particular dialog; their expectations are partly based on their image of what functions are in process. In particular, when a PILOT program is playing the part of a conversational partner, its responses can sometimes appear to be too rapid. Although, in general, users do not want to be delayed in their progress, there are times when brief pauses after responses may be more welcome than instantaneous reactions.

SUMMARY

Develop your program by first describing the overall results you wish to achieve. Create an outline in natural language, without concern for the rules of PILOT.

Next, convert your program sketch into PILOT using T: statements freely to describe something more complicated that you haven't yet written in detail. These "stubs" can later be turned into R: statements as the heading to a program module or subroutine. Keep your program runnable, even though it is incomplete.

The JM: statement was introduced as a brief way to program a multi-way jump, depending on which item in a preceding M: statement was matched.

When you find that the same operation occurs in several places or that there is a logical section of your program that can be given a meaningful name, create a module by placing a label at the beginning and an E: statement at the end of the section. You then call upon a particular module by writing a U: statement that refers to the label.

When your program becomes too large to fit into the available memory at one time, set aside a section of the program as a separate file and use the LOAD: statement to put that section into operation. The LOAD: statement causes the separate file to overlay (replace) the program that begins the operation.

As a program author, you must be concerned with how your program displays information and prompts the user to respond. Try to keep displays simple, and provide headings or titles where appropriate. The choices presented to a user can be repeated as headings when the chosen section begins. Since users have different needs as they become more skilled, your program should be able to adapt to their increased skill, perhaps skipping over full explanations, or using abbreviations or a more rapid operation than would be appropriate for a novice.

PILOT SESSION QUIZ

```
list
R: CHAPTER 5 QUIZ
CH:
CA: 10
T: These are some questions related to Chapter 5.
T:
T:          They are written in PILOT.
FOOT:
CH:
```

*Q1

T: "CURSOR" refers to:

:   1.   someone who swears.

:   2.   a careless expression.

:   3.   a marker on a display screen.

:   4.   letters connected together.

:

*Q1A

CA: 7

T: Choose a number \

CE:

A: #A

M: 1

Y: If there were such a word, it would probably be "curser."

JY: Q1B

M: 2

Y: Perhaps you are thinking of "cursory."

JY: Q1B

M: 3

Y: That's the best choice when talking about computers.

PAY: 10

JY: Q2

M: 4

Y: Maybe you mean "cursive."

JY: Q1B

N: Choose 1-4, please.

*Q1B T: Try again.

PA: 10

J: Q1A

*Q2

CH:

T: The following is an example of a brief _____.

:

:   *MOVEUP

:   R: Variables R and C are used for cursor position.

:   C: R=R-1

:   CA (R) : R, C

:   E

```
CA: 1, 40
A:
M:  subroutine,  module
CA: 9
Y: That's  the  right  word.
N: I  was  thinking  of  "subroutine"  or  "module."
T:
T: PRESS  "RETURN"  TO  CONTINUE
A:


*Q3
T: To  move  the  cursor  up  one  line,  a  program  could  use  this
 : module  with  the  statement  "U: MOVEUP".
 :    Is  that  True  or  False ?   (T/F)
A:
M:  T
Y: Yes,  as  long  as  R  was  already  at  the  cursor's  line  number.
N: "U: MOVEUP"  should  cause  use  of  the  module,  and  move  up  one  line.
FOOT:


*Q4 CH:
T: In  PILOT,  a  module  begins  with  a  _____  and  ends  with  _____.
CA: 1, 38
INMAX: 5
A: $ANS1
INMAX: 80
CA: 1, 58
A: $ANS2
M:  E
JN: Q4NO
A: =$ANS1
M: LABEL, *, ASTER
Y: Very  good,  right  on  both  counts.
FOOTY:
JY: Q5
*Q4NO
T: A  module  begins  with  a  label  and  ends  with  E:
FOOT:
```

84

*Q5 CH:

T: A "STUB" is:

:   1. a nickname for a stubborn person.

:   2. a short and thick section of program.

:   3. an ache in one's toe.

:   4. a comment printed in place of incomplete program code.

CA: 7

T: Choose a number \

A: #A

M: 4

Y: Yes, that's what it often means among programmers.

N: No, I use it to mean a temporary substitute for part of a
 : program that is not yet complete.

FOOT:

*Q6 CH:

T: The M: statement followed by JM: can replace a sequence of:

:   1. M:

:   JY:

:   M:

:   JY:

:   2. M:

:   JY:

:   MN:

:   JY:

:   3. M:

:   JN:

:   M:

:   JN:

:   4. 1 and 2

:   5. 2 and 3

:   6. 1 and 3

:   7. 1, 2, and 3

A: #A

M: 4

Y: Right.

T: The sequences in both 1 and 2 can be replaced by M: plus JM:
 : The sequence in 3 does something else, responding to "nomatch".

 :

FOOT: That's all for this quiz. Press RETURN to exit.

85

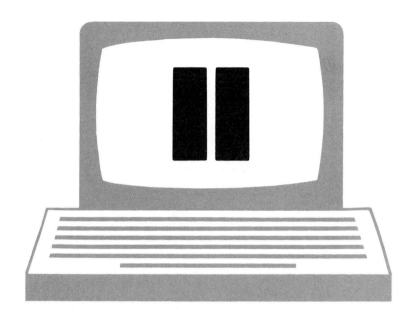

PROGRAMMING DIFFERENT TYPES OF CONVERSATIONS

In each of the following chapters, program segment examples will be given, alternative programming methods shown, and exercises provided for the reader to explore with an operational PILOT system. Although in an interactive situation there is an interplay of question and answer and a giving and gathering of information, chapters are organized by program emphasis. Chapter 6 describes drill and tutorial methods of giving information. Chapter 7 explores data collection, the gathering of information. Chapter 8 gives examples of quizzes and examinations. Chapter 9 features programs that involve the user in a simulation of a problem situation.

Giving information

DRILL EXERCISES

By this time, you should have no difficulty in designing an interaction providing a drill of specific facts, similar to the use of flash cards. Many drills are regular and repetitive in the overall structure, with only specific content changing from one question to the next. In this case, much of the repetitive portion can be separated into a module that is used over and over. In the following example, each question takes only three lines: the question to be asked, storage of the correct answer to be matched, and a call to the module.

Sometimes it is useful to work out the structure as a general case without reference to the specific content. Here is an example of such a structure, shown with two meaningless questions and a module used by both.

```
list
T: question one
C: $ans = 111
U: score

T: question 2
C: $ans = 222
U: score
E:
```

```
*score
A:
C: $ans
Y: Right
N: No, the answer is $ans
FOOT:
CH:
E:
```

The above is enough content to allow testing of the procedure. Once it is working to your satisfaction, the module can be left alone and you can plug the content into as many questions as you need. Thus, using the same module, you could write:

list
```
T: How many pints are in a quart?
C: $ans= 2
U: score

T: How many centimeters are in an inch?
C: $ans= 2.54
U: score

T: How many feet are in a mile?
C: $ans= 5280
U: score

T: A hammer and a saw are both _____.
 : (Type a single word)
C: $ans= tools
U: score

T: East and north are both _____.
 : (Type a single word)
C: $ans= directions
U: score
E:
```

You can see that the use of the module "score" has saved a lot of repetitive typing, leaving only the essentials to be entered for each question. The module "score" lets you create a *template* for this particular type of question. Whenever there are repetitive elements in a series of test questions, it is likely that you can benefit by collecting them in a module and using them with a brief U: statement. Referring to the previous example, if we chose to put all questions in a "fill-in" form (see the last two units), then the T: statement "(Type a single word)" could be included as the first line of the "score" module.

A programming note: When the U: statement is executed, some PILOT systems search for the label from the beginning of the program file. This can cause a sluggish response if the module is at the end of a long program; this condition can be avoided by placing the module near the beginning.

The following is a more complex example of a program designed to drill students at the second- or third-grade level in spelling. It uses modules to create specialized functions for accepting a letter in the right spot on the screen, testing if a letter is correct or if help is needed, and in resetting counters and other elements in preparation for a new word. Many R: statements are inserted to describe what is being accomplished.

A Spelling Drill

```
list
    R: SPELLING    Written by K. ANDERSON & S. WILLIAMS
J: *START
        R: JUMP TO START. MODULES ARE AT THE BEGINING SO THAT
        R: U: 'S WILL BE FASTER.


*A R: ACCEPT A LETTER
    CA: R, C
        R: SENTENCE IS ON ROW R, LETTER ON COLUMN C
T: .
        R: BLANK THAT POSITION
    CA: R, C
        R: BACK TO POSITION
```

INMAX: 1

A:

    R: GET LETTER

E:

*T R: TEST IF A LETTER IS CORRECT OR IF HELP IS NEEDED

  CA: R, C

    R: PUT CURSOR IN POSITION

CY: E=-2

    R: RESET ERROR COUNTER (IF LETTER CORRECT)

CY: C=C+1

    R: SET COLUMN FOR NEXT LETTER (IF LETTER CORRECT)

EY:

    R: RETURN (IF LETTER CORRECT)

M: ?,

    R: TEST IF HELP NEEDED

    R: INDICATE LETTER WRONG (OR HELP)

CN: E=E+1

    R: INCREMENT ERROR COUNTER

M(E): ,

    R: IF THREE ERRORS THEN HELP

EN:

    R: RETURN IF NOT HELPING

C: H=H+1

    R: COUNT HOW MANY TIMES HELPED

C: E=-2

    R: RESET ERROR COUNTER

C: C=C+1

    R: SET COLUMN FOR NEXT LETTER

E:

*I R: INITIALIZATION FOR EACH WORD

  CH:

    R: CLEAR THE SCREEN

C: R=5

    R: START ON ROW FIVE

  CA: R

    R: PUT CURSOR THERE

```
C: H=0
       R: RESET HELP COUNT
C: E=-2
       R: RESET ERROR COUNTER
E:


*R  R: TEST FOR RE-TRY
M:  ,
       R: SET MATCH FLAG TO "YES"
C: T=H-1
       R: TEST IF H>1
T(T): I HAD TO HELP YOU #H TIMES ON THAT ONE, LET'S TRY IT AGAIN.
C: T=-T
       R: TEST IF H<1
E(T):
       R: RETURN IF H<1
C: T=T+1
       R: TEST IF H=1
T(T): I HAD TO HELP YOU ON THAT ONE, LET'S TRY IT AGAIN.
A:
       R: WAIT FOR ENTRY
M: **
       R: ERRORS, SO SET MATCH FLAG TO "NO"
E:


*START
  CH:
  CA: 3
T: I WILL SHOW YOU A SENTENCE WITH A WORD MISSING
 : AND YOU FILL IN THE MISSING WORD.
 : I WILL GIVE YOU THE FIRST LETTER OF THE WORD.
 : IF YOU HAVE NOT GOTTEN A LETTER ON THE THIRD TRY,
 : I WILL GIVE YOU THE LETTER.
 : I WILL ALSO HELP YOU IF YOU TYPE A "?"
 : IF I HAVE TO HELP YOU, I WILL USE THE SAME WORD OVER.
 : PRESS "RETURN" TO GO ON.
A:
```

```
*W1 U:*I
     R: TRY FIRST WORD
T: THE DAY AFTER MONDAY IS T_ _ _ _ _ _.
C: C=26
     R: WORD STARTS ON COLUMN 26
*1A U:*A
     R: GET FIRST LETTER
M: U
     R: MATCH WITH CORRECT LETTER
U: *T
     R: TEST IF CORRECT, HELP, ETC.
JN: *1A
     R: JUMP TO RE-TRY THE LETTER (IF WRONG)
T: U
     R: TYPE THE LETTER
*1B U:*A
M: E
U: *T
JN: *1B
T: E
*1C U:*A
M: S
U: *T
JN: *1C
T: S
*1D U:*A
M: D
U: *T
JN: *1D
T: DAY
U: *R
JN: *W1
T: VERY GOOD! LET'S TRY ANOTHER WORD.
A:


*W2 U:*I
T: DO YOU KNOW THE A_ _ _ _ _ TO THE QUESTION?
C: C=18
```

```
*2N  U: *A
M: N
U: *T
JN: *2N
T: N
*2S  U: *A
M: S
U: *T
JN: *2S
T: S
*2W  U: *A
M: W
U: *T
JN: *2W
T: W
*2E  U: *A
M: E
U: *T
JN: *2E
T: E
*2R  U: *A
M: R
U: *T
JN: *2R
T: R
U: *R
JN: *W2
T: GREAT!  LET'S TRY ANOTHER ONE.
A:

*W3  U: *I
T: GRASS IS GREEN AND THE SKY IS B_ _ _.
C: C=32
*3L  U: *A
M: L
U: *T
JN: *3L
T: L
```

*3U U: *A
M: U
U: *T
JN: *3U
T: U
*3E U: *A
M: E
U: *T
JN: *3E
T: E
U: *R
JN: *W3
T: VERY GOOD!
A:

*W4 U: *I
T: WHEN YOU ARE BAD, YOU GET IN T_ _ _ _ _ _.
C: C=31
*4R U: *A
M: R
U: *T
JN: *4R
T: R
*4O U: *A
M: O
U: *T
JN: *4O
T: O
*4U U: *A
M: U
U: *T
JN: *4U
T: U
*4B U: *A
M: B
U: *T
JN: *4B
T: B

*4L U: *A
M: L
U: *T
JN: *4L
T: L
*4E U: *A
M: E
U: *T
JN: *4E
T: E
U: *R
JN: *W4
T: GOOD, LET'S TRY ANOTHER DAY OF THE WEEK.
A:

*W5 U: *I
T: THE DAY BEFORE THURSDAY IS W_ _ _ _ _ _ _ _.
C: C=29
*5A U: *A
M: E
U: *T
JN: *5A
T: E
*5B U: *A
M: D
U: *T
JN: *5B
T: D
*5N U: *A
M: N
U: *T
JN: *5N
T: N
*5E U: *A
M: E
U: *T
JN: *5E
T: E

*5S U: *A
M: S
U: *T
JN: *5S
T: S
*5D U: *A
M: D
U: *T
JN: *5D
T: DAY
U: *R
JN: *W5
T: GOOD!
A:

*W6 U: *I
T: YOU GO TO THE D_ _ _ _ _ WHEN YOU ARE SICK.
C: C=16
*6A U: *A
M: O
U: *T
JN: *6A
T: O
*6C U: *A
M: C
U: *T
JN: *6C
T: C
*6T U: *A
M: T
U: *T
JN: *6T
T: T
*6O U: *A
M: O
U: *T
JN: *6O
T: O

```
*6R U: *A
M: R
U: *T
JN: *6R
T: R
U: *R
JN: *W6
T: GREAT!
A:


*W7 U: *I
T: YELLOW IS A BRIGHT C_ _ _ _.
C: C=21
*7A U: *A
M: O
U: *T
JN: *7A
T: O
*7L U: *A
M: L
U: *T
JN: *7L
T: L
*7O U: *A
M: O
U: *T
JN: *7O
T: O
*7R U: *A
M: R
U: *T
JN: *7R
T: R
U: *R
JN: *W7
T: YOU'RE DOING VERY WELL!
A:
```

*W8 U: *I
T: THERE ARE SEVEN DAYS IN A W_ _ _.
C: C=28
*8A U: *A
M: E
U: *T
JN: *8A
T: E
*8E U: *A
M: E
U: *T
JN: *8E
T: E
*8K U: *A
M: K
U: *T
JN: *8K
T: K
U: *R
JN: *W8
T: GOOD!
A:

*W9 U: *I
T: YOU GO TO THE STORE TO B_ _ THINGS.
C: C=25
*9U U: *A
M: U
U: *T
JN: *9U
T: U
*9Y U: *A
M: Y
U: *T
JN: *9Y
T: Y
U: *R

JN: *W9
T: GOOD!
A:

*W10 U: *I
T: WHAT IS ONE PLUS ONE? T_ _.
C: C=24
*10W U: *A
M: W
U: *T
JN: *10W
T: W
*10O U: *A
M: O
U: *T
JN: *10O
T: O
U: *R
JN: *W10
T: VERY GOOD!
A:

*W11 U: *I
T: SOME STORIES START WITH "O_ _ _ UPON A TIME...."
C: C=27
*11N U: *A
M: N
U: *T
JN: *11N
T: N
*11C U: *A
M: C
U: *T
JN: *11C
T: C
*11E U: *A
M: E
U: *T

```
JN: *11E
T: E
U: *R
JN: *W11
T: YOU ARE DOING VERY WELL!
A:

*W12  U: *I
T: THE SECOND MONTH OF THE YEAR IS F_ _ _ _ _ _ _ .
C: C=34
*12E  U: *A
M: E
U: *T
JN: *12E
T: E
*12B  U: *A
M: B
U: *T
JN: *12B
T: B
*12R  U: *A
M: R
U: *T
JN: *12R
T: R
*12U  U: *A
M: U
U: *T
JN: *12U
T: U
*12A  U: *A
M: A
U: *T
JN: *12A
T: A
*12X  U: *A
M: R
U: *T
```

JN: *12X
T: R
*12Y U: *A
M: Y
U: *T
JN: *12Y
T: Y
U: *R
JN: *W12
T: VERY GOOD , THAT WAS A HARD ONE!
A:

*W13 U: *I
T: A PENCIL IS USED TO W_ _ _ _ ON A PIECE OF PAPER.
C: C=22
*13R U: *A
M: R
U: *T
JN: *13R
T: R
*13I U: *A
M: I
U: *T
JN: *13I
T: I
*13T U: *A
M: T
U: *T
JN: *13T
T: T
*13E U: *A
M: E
U: *T
JN: *13E
T: E
U: *R
JN: *W13
T: VERY GOOD!
A:

104

*W14 U: *I
T: TO FIND OUT WHAT A BOOK SAYS , YOU R_ _ _ IT.
C: C=36
*14E U: *A
M: E
U: *T
JN: *14E
T: E
*14A U: *A
M: A
U: *T
JN: *14A
T: A
*14D U: *A
M: D
U: *T
JN: *14D
T: D
U: *R
JN: *W14
T: GOOD , LET'S GO ON.
A:

*W15 U: *I
T: YOU USE YOUR EARS TO H_ _ _ SOUNDS.
C: C=23
*15E U: *A
M: E
U: *T
JN: *15E
T: E
*15A U: *A
M: A
U: *T
JN: *15A
T: A
*15R U: *A
M: R
U: *T

JN: *15R
T: R
U: *R
JN: *W15
T: GOOD!
A:

*W16 U: *I
T: S_ _ _ _ IS VERY SWEET.
C: C=2
*16U U: *A
M: U
U: *T
JN: *16U
T: U
*16G U: *A
M: G
U: *T
JN: *16G
T: G
*16A U: *A
M: A
U: *T
JN: *16A
T: A
*16R U: *A
M: R
U: *T
JN: *16R
T: R
U: *R
JN: *W16
T: VERY GOOD!
A:

*W17 U: *I
T: YOU WEAR S_ _ _ _ ON YOUR FEET.
C: C=11

*17H U: *A
M: H
U: *T
JN: *17H
T: H
*17O U: *A
M: O
U: *T
JN: *17O
T: O
*17E U: *A
M: E
U: *T
JN: *17E
T: E
*17S U: *A
M: S
U: *T
JN: *17S
T: S
U: *R
JN: *W17
T: YOU'RE DOING GREAT!
A:

*W18 U: *I
T: THE NUMBER AFTER THIRTY-NINE IS F_ _ _ _.
C: C=34
*18O U: *A
M: O
U: *T
JN: *18O
T: O
*18R U: *A
M: R
U: *T
JN: 18R
T: R

```
*18T U: *A
M: T
U: *T
JN: *18T
T: T
*18Y U: *A
M: Y
U: *T
JN: *18Y
T: Y
U: *R
JN: *W18
T: GREAT!
A:


*W19 U: *I
T: SOME  WORDS  ARE  HARD  TO  SPELL  , AND  SOME  ARE  E_ _ _.
C: C=45
*19A U: *A
M: A
U: *T
JN: *19A
T: A
*19S U: *A
M: S
U: *T
JN: *19S
T: S
*19Y U: *A
M: Y
U: *T
JN: *19Y
T: Y
U: *R
JN: *W19
T: VERY GOOD!
A:
```

*W20 U: *I
T: WORKING HARD CAN MAKE YOU T_ _ _ _.
C: C=28
*20I U: *A
M: I
U: *T
JN: *20I
T: I
*20R U: *A
M: R
U: *T
JN: *20R
T: R
*20E U: *A
M: E
U: *T
JN: *20E
T: E
*20D U: *A
M: D
U: *T
JN: *20D
T: D
U: *R
JN: *W20
T: YOU ARE DOING VERY WELL , YOU HAVE DONE TWENTY WORDS.
A:

*W21 U: *I
T: DO YOU K_ _ _ HOW TO SPELL THIS WORD?
C: C=9
*21N U: *A
M: N
U: *T
JN: *21N
T: N
*21O U: *A
M: O

U: *T
JN: *21O
T: O
*21W U: *A
M: W
U: *T
JN: *21W
T: W
U: *R
JN: *W21
T: YOU DO!
A:

*W22 U: *I
T: THE UNITED STATES IS THE C_ _ _ _ _ _ WE LIVE IN.
C: C=27
*22O U: *A
M: O
U: *T
JN: *22O
T: O
*22U U: *A
M: U
U: *T
JN: *22U
T: U
*22N U: *A
M: N
U: *T
JN: *22N
T: N
*22T U: *A
M: T
U: *T
JN: *22T
T: T
*22R U: *A
M: R

U: *T
JN: *22R
T: R
*22Y U: *A
M: Y
U: *T
JN: *22Y
T: Y
U: *R
JN: *W22
T: VERY GOOD!
A:

*W23 U: *I
T: GLASS DROPPED ON A HARD FLOOR IS LIKELY TO B_ _ _.
C: C=45
*23R U: *A
M: R
U: *T
JN: *23R
T: R
*23E U: *A
M: E
U: *T
JN: *23E
T: E
*23A U: *A
M: A
U: *T
JN: *23A
T: A
*23K U: *A
M: K
U: *T
JN: *23K
T: K
U: *R
JN: *W23

```
T: AND IT WILL MAKE A BIG MESS.
A:
T:
T: THAT'S ALL FOR NOW.
PA: 3
E:
```

This example exhibits some good characteristics for a drill and practice program aimed at elementary students. It is unusual in providing a response to every key press (this would not be appropriate for a rapid typist but is acceptable in this context). Students are given clear instructions and prompts along the way, with the assumption that they have no previous knowledge about the computer. Feedback for correct and incorrect responses is immediate and clear, and students can proceed at whatever pace is comfortable for them. A further elaboration might be to keep a record of overall scores so students can see a summary of their performance.

From the instructor's standpoint, the use of modules makes it relatively simple to create a version with different words or to just change the content of this example. For extensive use, a program of this type could be written to obtain lists of words from a disk file. The instructor would need only to create a simple word list in order to change the content.

An Algebra Drill

Since PILOT can evaluate algebraic expressions dealing with integers, it can provide practice in basic algebra. This is illustrated in the following brief program.

```
list
CH:
T:  HERE IS AN ALGEBRA PROBLEM FOR YOU.
 :  YOU GIVE ME A NUMBER, AND I WILL USE IT IN A PROBLEM I
 :  HAVE FOR YOU. HERE WE GO.
 :  ENTER A NUMBER THAT WE'LL CALL.N IN THIS EQUATION.
 :
```

```
:      X = (10-N)+(N*2)
:
A: #N
T:
T: OK, HERE'S HOW IT LOOKS WITH YOUR NUMBER.
T: NOW YOU SOLVE THE EQUATION FOR X.
:
T:      X = (10-#N)+(#N*2)
:
: WHEN READY, ENTER THE VALUE OF X.
:
A: #X
T:
C: Y=(10-N)+(N*2)
T(X=Y): RIGHT, YOU GOT IT!
T(X<>Y): TOO BAD, YOU MISSED IT.
E:
```

After this program accepts a number from the student, it first substitutes the number in the equation so that the student is certain about what is to be evaluated. It then asks for the answer to be entered. A PILOT C: statement then substitutes the number and evaluates the expression, storing the result in Y. The values of X and Y can then be compared to make operation of the following T: statements conditional. This is the first example of this relational term in parentheses that was described at the end of Chapter 3.

Here is what the program looks like when it runs:

run
```
HERE IS AN ALGEBRA PROBLEM FOR YOU.
YOU GIVE ME A NUMBER, AND I WILL USE IT IN A PROBLEM I
HAVE FOR YOU. HERE WE GO.
ENTER A NUMBER THAT WE'LL CALL N IN THIS EQUATION.


        X = (10-N)+(N*2)
```

OK, HERE'S HOW IT LOOKS WITH YOUR NUMBER.
NOW YOU SOLVE THE EQUATION FOR X.

$$X = (10-8) + (8*2)$$

WHEN READY, ENTER THE VALUE OF X.

18

RIGHT, YOU GOT IT!

READY

This sample program should give you some ideas with which to make a variety of drills for arithmetic or algebra. Another way to add variety to numeric programs of this type is to introduce a random number. In the sample program, for example, a random number in the range of 1 to 10 (whatever number you choose) might replace entry of a number by the student. Or a random number might be used to replace the constants in the equation. One variation that replaces the constants with RND(10) is this:

```
CH:
T: HERE IS AN ALGEBRA PROBLEM FOR YOU.
 : YOU GIVE ME A NUMBER, AND I WILL USE IT IN A PROBLEM I
 : HAVE FOR YOU. HERE WE GO.
 : ENTER A NUMBER THAT WE'LL CALL N IN THIS EQUATION.
 : I WILL CHOOSE VALUES FOR A AND B.
 :
 :      X = (A-N) + (N*B)
```

```
:
A: #N
T:
T: OK, HERE'S HOW IT LOOKS WITH YOUR NUMBER.
T:     NOW YOU SOLVE THE EQUATION FOR X.
:
   C: A=RND(10)
   C: B=RND(10)
T:     X = (#A-#N)+(#N*#B)
:
: WHEN READY, ENTER THE VALUE OF X.
:
A: #X
T:
C:  Y=(A-N)+(N*B)
T(X=Y): RIGHT, YOU GOT IT!
T(X<>Y): TOO BAD, YOU MISSED IT.
```

This makes the drill problems a little more interesting.

TUTORIAL INTERACTION

If you were to present information in an organized fashion but without interaction, there would be little reason to make use of a computer system. PILOT makes it easy to not only display the information that you wish, but also to ask questions along the way and obtain feedback to indicate whether or not the information is being understood or whether further explanation is required. Such feedback can be collected and used to improve a lesson for students in the future.

The functions required to make your first draft of an instructional sequence need not be complex. The following is a brief tutorial example created by a student when first learning PILOT.

list
```
R: English tea.  Written by Mary Lough.
```

CH:

T: This program will teach you how to make a perfect cup of
: English tea.

T: Do you like to drink tea?

T: Please answer y (yes) or n (no).

A:

M: y

TY: Great! The following steps should be easy for you.

TN: That is O.K. This will teach you the steps in case you have a
: guest who likes to drink tea.

T: Please type in your first name, and then press return to
: continue.

A: $name

T: Thank you $name.
: Imagine that you are in an English cottage and you have just
: decided to make a cup of afternoon tea. The first thing that
: you will do is:
:
: a. Pour hot water from the tap into a cup with a teabag?
: b. Pour cold water into a kettle?
: c. Pour cold water into a cup with a teabag?
:
: Please choose one of the options above by pressing a, b, or c.

A:

M: a

TN: No, most people in England heat cold water for tea.
:

T: Now imagine that you have put the water on to heat. Since "a
: watched pot never boils," take five minutes to admire the view
: from the cottage window.
:

PA: 5

T: The water has been on the stove for a while. At what point
: will you remove it from the stove?
:
: a. When it has heated for five minutes.
: b. When it is boiling, and there are bubbles in the water.
: c. When it is lukewarm.

116

```
    :
    : Please answer a, b, or c.
A:
M: b
T:
TY: That's right. You must have boiling water to infuse tea
    : properly.
TN: No, that's not quite right. If the water is not boiling, tea
    : tastes like dishwater.
    :
T: Once the water has boiled, you should heat the teapot before
    : putting in the tea and pouring the boiling water into it. This
    : is more important with a ceramic teapot than one made of metal.
    :
    : Now that the tea leaves are infusing, how long should you leave
    : them to brew?
    :
    : a. 1 to 2 minutes.
    : b. 3 to 5 minutes.
    : c. more than 5 minutes.
    :
    : Answer a, b, or c.
A:
M: b
T:
TY: Correct. 3 to 5 minutes will bring out flavour without too
    : strong a taste.
TN: Sorry, 3 to 5 minutes will bring out the best flavour of the
    : tea.
T: Thank you, $name. I hope that you enjoy your cup of tea.
E:


run
    This program will teach you how to make a perfect cup of
    English tea.
    Do you like to drink tea?
    Please answer y (yes) or n (no).
```

y

Great! The following steps should be easy for you.
Please type in your first name, and then press return to
continue.

John

Thank you John.
Imagine that you are in an English cottage and you have just
decided to make a cup of afternoon tea. The first thing that
you will do is:

a. Pour hot water from the tap into a cup with a teabag?
b. Pour cold water into a kettle?
c. Pour cold water into a cup with a teabag?

Please choose one of the options above, by pressing a, b, or c.

a

No, most people in England heat cold water for tea.

Now imagine that you have put the water on to heat. Since "a
watched pot never boils," take five minutes to admire the view
from the cottage window.

The water has been on the stove for a while. At what point
will you remove it from the stove?

a. When it has heated for five minutes.
b. When it is boiling, and there are bubbles in the water.
c. When it is lukewarm.

Please answer a, b, or c.

b

That's right. You must have boiling water to infuse tea
properly.
Once the water has boiled, you should heat the teapot before
putting in the tea and pouring the boiling water into it. This
is more important with a ceramic teapot than one made of metal.

Now that the tea leaves are infusing, how long should you leave
them to brew?

118

a. 1 to 2 minutes.
b. 3 to 5 minutes.
c. more than 5 minutes.

Answer a, b, or c.
b

Correct. 3 to 5 minutes will bring out flavour without too strong a taste.
Thank you, John. I hope that you enjoy your cup of tea.

The provision of information can often be supplemented by the opportunity to ask a question or two in order to meet specific needs. For example, here is another student product:

list
R: Swimming schedules.   Written by Peggy Dolcini.
T: Welcome to SWIMTIME!
:
: SWIMTIME provides information about the days and times the
: recreation center swimming pool is open.
: Please answer the following questions to determine how your
: schedule and the pool's schedule mesh.
:
: Do you want to swim in the morning?
A:
M: yes
TY: The pool is open every weekday at 7:30 am. It is not open on
: Saturday or Sunday mornings. On Friday, it closes from 9:00 to
: 11:00.
EY:
T: Well then, do you want to swim in the afternoon?
A:
M: yes
TY: The pool is CLOSED during the following times:
: Tuesdays and Thursdays from 2:30 to 4:00.
: Saturdays and Sundays from 4:30 to 5:30.
: At all other times, it is open during the afternoon.
EY:

T: If you don't want to swim in the morning or in the afternoon,
: do you want to swim in the evening?
A:
M: yes
TY: The pool is open until 6:45 on Monday and Wednesday.
: Tuesdays and Thursdays it remains open until 9:00.
: Fridays and Saturdays it is open until 8:00.
: Sundays it is open until 7:00.
EY:
T: You must not want to swim.
E:

run
Welcome to SWIMTIME!

SWIMTIME provides information about the days and times the
recreation center swimming pool is open.
Please answer the following questions to determine how your
schedule and the pool's schedule mesh.

Do you want to swim in the morning?
no
Well then, do you want to swim in the afternoon?
yes
The pool is CLOSED during the following times:
Tuesdays and Thursdays from 2:30 to 4:00.
Saturdays and Sundays from 4:30 to 5:30.
At all other times, it is open during the afternoon.

READY
run
Welcome to SWIMTIME!

SWIMTIME provides information about the days and times the
recreation center swimming pool is open.
Please answer the following questions to determine how your
schedule and the pool's schedule mesh.

Do you want to swim in the morning?

no

Well then, do you want to swim in the afternoon?

no

If you don't want to swim in the morning or in the afternoon,
do you want to swim in the evening?

yes

The pool is open until 6:45 on Monday and Wednesday.
Tuesdays and Thursdays it remains open until 9:00.
Fridays and Saturdays it is open until 8:00.
Sundays it is open until 7:00.

READY

This program simply terminates after providing the requested information. In the context of a more extensive interaction, the EY: statements might become JY: statements, jumping to a common continuation point.

Tutorial sequences often amount to brief presentations followed by tests of comprehension. In the following student program, a chance is provided for review of part of the original presentation.

list

R: Developmental theory.   Written by Mary McCall.
CH:
*INTRO T:Erik Erikson is a therapist as well as a researcher and
:theorist in the field of human development. His well-known theory
:of lifespan development is our topic of discussion in this
:segment of PILOT. Erikson described development of the ego, or
:psychosocial self, in terms of eight "crises" or stages, with polar
:outcomes for the ego and how one feels about oneself. These
:outcomes also influence how the ego deals with the next crisis—
:the ego strength available to the individual. Before discussing
:these polarities in further detail, however, let's get more
:familiar with the eight stages and their polar outcomes.
U: *STAGES

```
*QUESTION1
CH:
T:  What is Erikson's first stage—what are the polarities?
A:
M:  trust
TY:  Great!
JY:  *QUESTION2
T:  Sorry, that is a little off. Why don't you try again?
A:
M:  trust
TY:  Good—you're on the right track now.
JY:  *QUESTION2
T:  Do you need to look at the list again?
A:
M:  yes, sure, ok, please
UY:  *STAGES
J:  *QUESTION1


*QUESTION2
T:  What is the last stage of Erikson's theory?
A:
M:  ego integrity
MY:  despair
TY:  You're doing wonderfully!
JY:  *QUESTION3
T:  Sorry—that's not entirely right—try again.
M:  ego integrity
MY:  despair
TY:  Good! Let's go on—
JY:  *QUESTION3
T:  Do you need to look at the list again?
A:
M:  yes, sure, ok, please
UY:  *STAGES
J:  *QUESTION2


*QUESTION3
T:  Okay, now let's go on to the next section.
```

T: What are the polarities that an adolescent might
 : deal with?
T: ..... (this is a temporary end)
E:

*STAGES T:
         : Stage 1—trust vs. mistrust
         : Stage 2—autonomy vs. shame and doubt
         : Stage 3—initiative vs. guilt
         : Stage 4—industry vs. inferiority
         : Stage 5—identity vs. role confusion
         : Stage 6—intimacy vs. isolation
         : Stage 7—generativity vs. stagnation
         : Stage 8—ego integrity vs. despair

:Now that we have looked at these for a while, let's take a
:little quiz on them. You will have a chance to look at this
:list of stages again if you need to. Press RETURN now.
A:
CH:
E:

run
Erik Erikson is a therapist as well as a researcher and
theorist in the field of human development. His well-known theory
of lifespan development is our topic of discussion in this
segment of PILOT. Erikson described development of the ego, or
psychosocial self, in terms of eight "crises" or stages, with polar
outcomes for the ego and how one feels about oneself. These
outcomes also influence how the ego deals with the next crisis—
the ego strength available to the individual. Before discussing
these polarities in further detail, however, let's get more
familiar with the eight stages and their polar outcomes.

 Stage 1—trust vs. mistrust
 Stage 2—autonomy vs. shame and doubt

Stage 3—initiative vs. guilt
Stage 4—industry vs. inferiority
Stage 5—identity vs. role confusion
Stage 6—intimacy vs. isolation
Stage 7—generativity vs. stagnation
Stage 8—ego integrity vs. despair

Now that we have looked at these for a while, let's take a little quiz on them. You will have a chance to look at this list of stages again if you need to. Press RETURN now.

What is Erikson's first stage—what are the polarities?
trust and mistrust
 Great!
 What is the last stage of Erikson's theory?
integrity?
 Sorry—that's not entirely right—try again.
ego integrity
 Do you need to look at the list again?
yes

Stage 1—trust vs. mistrust
Stage 2—autonomy vs. shame and doubt
Stage 3—initiative vs. guilt
Stage 4—industry vs. inferiority
Stage 5—identity vs. role confusion
Stage 6—intimacy vs. isolation
Stage 7—generativity vs. stagnation
Stage 8—ego integrity vs. despair

Now that we have looked at these for a while, let's take a little quiz on them. You will have a chance to look at this list of stages again if you need to. Press RETURN now.

What is the last stage of Erikson's theory?

ego integrity vs. despair
You're doing wonderfully!
Okay, now let's go on to the next section.
What are the polarities that an adolescent might deal with?
..... (this is a temporary end)

Gathering Information

SIMPLE PROMPTING
FOR DATA COLLECTION

For many applications, it is sufficient to prompt for an entry, accept an answer, save it, and go on to the next prompt. For example:

```
list
*START
T: Please enter your last name.
A: $lname
T: Enter your first name.
A: $fname
    R: We can check on its accuracy here.
T: Your name is entered as "$fname $lname"
 : Is that correct?
A:
M: Y
N: Let's try again.
JN: START
T: Next entry _ _ _
```

Let's apply this simple data collection to the creation of a common parlor game. One person asks the others in a group to supply nouns, adjectives, adverbs, or exclamations sufficient to fill in the blanks in a story that they haven't seen. After all the data has been supplied, the story is read with often amusing results. The following shows you how easy it is to collect data in PILOT.

list

```
T: If you supply me with some nouns, adjectives, and adverbs, I
 : will use them to tell you a story that you might find amusing.
 : First, tell me the name of a man that you know fairly well.
 : Just the first name will do.
A: $name
T: Think of some nouns (names of things).
T: I need four of them, so enter the first.
A: $noun1
T: Now a second one,
A: $noun2
T: and a third,
A: $noun3
T: and one more.
A: $noun4
T: I also need the name of a place.
A: $place
T: Now enter a plural noun.
A: $pnoun1
T: Now think of adjectives (that describe something or somebody).
 : I need four of those.
 : Just press RETURN after each one.
A: $adj1
A: $adj2
A: $adj3
A: $adj4
T: Now for some adverbs (that tell how something is done; they will
 : usually end in "ly"). I need two.
A: $adv1
A: $adv2
T: Thank you.
 :
T: When you are ready to appreciate the story you have helped
 : write, press the RETURN key.
```

R: An A: statement is used to wait until the user is ready.
```
A:
CH:
T:           When $name Got Most Excited
 :
: $name left work on Friday night after a $adj1 week and started
: to drive to $place. His car was acting $adj2 but it was running
: $adv1. There were lots of $pnoun1 in the car with him so no
: wonder he was $adj3. Events went from bad to worse as he saw a
: $noun1 in the street and ran his $noun2 into it. A $adj4 lady
: tried to hit him with her $noun3 and he $adv2 escaped. He had
: no more $noun4 by the time he reached home.
: Well, that's all I heard about it.
E:
```

Here is how one person ran the program:

run
If you supply me with some nouns, adjectives, and adverbs, I
will use them to tell you a story that you might find amusing.
First, tell me the name of a man that you know fairly well.
Just the first name will do.
Ralph
Think of some nouns (names of things).
I need four of them, so enter the first.
horse
Now a second one,
umbrella
and a third,
book
and one more.
suitcase
I also need the name of a place.
San Jose
Now enter a plural noun.
turkeys
Now think of adjectives (that describe something or somebody).
I need four of those.

Just press RETURN after each one.
sad
indecent
angry
stupid
Now for some adverbs (that tell how something is done; they will usually end in "ly"). I need two.
carefully
loudly
Thank you.

When you are ready to appreciate the story you have helped write, press the RETURN key.

                    When Ralph Got Most Excited

Ralph left work on Friday night after a sad week and started to drive to San Jose. His car was acting indecent but it was running carefully. There were lots of turkeys in the car with him so no wonder he was angry. Events went from bad to worse as he saw a horse in the street and ran his umbrella into it. A stupid lady tried to hit him with her book and he loudly escaped. He had no more suitcase by the time he reached home.
   Well, that's all I heard about it.

You can try the program with some friends, but it may be even more fun to rewrite the program around your own story line. You can probably make up a better fill-in story than this.

You can also take a fairy tale or a nursery rhyme and prompt the user of your program to provide important elements. At about the time that PILOT was first being designed, some children had a good time designing ways to modify well-known stories like Goldilocks and the Three Bears. Here is an example of gathering ideas from the program user in order to add interest to the story.

list

R: GOLDILOCKS. Written by Dean Brown and children.

R: Modified by J. Starkweather, 1973.

CH:

T: YOU CAN REWRITE THE STORY OF GOLDILOCKS AND THE THREE BEARS.

  :

  : WHEN THE COMPUTER STOPS, IT IS YOUR TURN TO WRITE

  : PART OF THE STORY.

  : IF YOU MAKE A MISTAKE, USE DELETE TO CANCEL A LETTER

  : OR CTL/X TO CANCEL THE LINE BEFORE "RETURN"

  : NOW-PRESS "RETURN" TO BEGIN

A:

CH:

T:

T: ONCE UPON A TIME, THERE WERE THREE BEARS.

TH: Who do you think they were?

A:

T:

T: GOLDILOCKS DIDN'T LIKE PORRIDGE SO SHE FOUND SOME FROOT

TH: LOOPS IN THE KITCHEN. What did she do?

A: $A4

M: SHE

T:

T: THEN THE THREE BEARS CAME HOME. THE LITTLE BEAR SNIFFED

TH: AROUND AND SAID...

A: $A1

CH:

T: "AH HAH! I SEE SOMEONE", HE SAID.

T:

T: THEN THE GREAT BIG DADDY BEAR CHASED GOLDILOCKS ALL OVER

  : THE HOUSE. HE DID IT BECAUSE WHEN SHE FOUND THE

TH: FROOT LOOPS

TY: $A4

TN: SHE $A4

T:

T: GOLDILOCKS HID UNDER THE BED.

  : BABY BEAR HID UNDER THE BED.

  : THEY SAT ON BABY BEAR'S ELECTRIC TRAIN. What happened?

A:

T: AND. . .

A:

CH:

T:

T: PRETTY SOON MAMA BEAR CAME IN SCREAMING,
 : "WHO ATE MY FROOT LOOPS ALL UP?"

TH: SOMEONE ANSWERED. . .

A:

T:

 : GOLDILOCKS LAUGHED.
 : BABY BEAR LAUGHED EVEN HARDER.
 : HE SAID "$A1."

TH: MAMA BEAR SAID. . .

A: $A3

CH:

T:

T: THEN THEY WENT ON A PICNIC.
 : THEY FILLED THE PICNIC BASKET WITH CHOCOLATE. . .
 : AND HOT DOGS. . .

TH: AND BUBBLE GUM AND. . .

A: $A2

T: AND POPSICLES AND PEANUT BUTTER AND JELLY.

T:

TH: THEY DECIDED TO GO TO. . .

A: $A5

CH:

T:

T: WHEN THEY GOT THERE, THE GREAT BIG DADDY BEAR OPENED THE
 : DOOR AND ALL OF THE $A2 FELL OUT OF THE CAR.
 :
 : THE BABY BEAR SAID "$A1."
 : THE MAMA BEAR SAID "$A3."

TH: THE GREAT BIG DADDY BEAR SAID. . .

A: $A6

CH:

T:

T: GOLDILOCKS BEGAN TO CRY. . .

```
: "I WANT TO LEAVE $A5.
:    I WANT TO GO HOME. "
:
: BUT THE CAR HAD A FLAT TIRE AND THEY ALL HAD TO SLEEP THAT
: NIGHT IN THE BACK SEAT, AND THE GREAT BIG DADDY BEAR
: GRUMBLED "$A6" ALL NIGHT LONG.
:
:
T: *** THE END ***
T:
: PRESS "RETURN" PLEASE
A:
E:
```

RUN

YOU CAN REWRITE THE STORY OF GOLDILOCKS AND THE THREE BEARS.

WHEN THE COMPUTER STOPS, IT IS YOUR TURN TO WRITE
    PART OF THE STORY.
IF YOU MAKE A MISTAKE, USE DELETE TO CANCEL A LETTER
 OR CTL/X TO CANCEL THE LINE BEFORE "RETURN"

NOW-PRESS "RETURN" TO BEGIN

ONCE UPON A TIME, THERE WERE THREE BEARS.
Who do you think they were? **ANDY, SAM, AND FRED**

GOLDILOCKS DIDN'T LIKE PORRIDGE SO SHE FOUND SOME FROOT
LOOPS IN THE KITCHEN. What did she do? **SHE ATE EVERY BIT**

THEN THE THREE BEARS CAME HOME. THE LITTLE BEAR SNIFFED
AROUND AND SAID.... **SOMEONE IS IN THIS HOUSE**
"AH HAH! I SEE SOMEONE", HE SAID.

THEN THE GREAT BIG DADDY BEAR CHASED GOLDILOCKS ALL OVER
THE HOUSE. HE DID IT BECAUSE WHEN SHE FOUND THE
FROOT LOOPS **SHE ATE EVERY BIT**

GOLDILOCKS HID UNDER THE BED.
BABY BEAR HID UNDER THE BED.
THEY SAT ON BABY BEAR'S ELECTRIC TRAIN. What happened?
THEY BROKE IT
AND...
THE WHISTLE KEPT BLOWING

PRETTY SOON MAMA BEAR CAME IN SCREAMING,
"WHO ATE MY FROOT LOOPS ALL UP?"
SOMEONE ANSWERED...**THEY TASTED SO GOOD**

GOLDILOCKS LAUGHED.
BABY BEAR LAUGHED EVEN HARDER.
HE SAID "SOMEONE IS IN THIS HOUSE."
MAMA BEAR SAID...**I BOUGHT THOSE FROOT LOOPS TO EAT MYSELF**

THEN THEY WENT ON A PICNIC.
THEY FILLED THE PICNIC BASKET WITH CHOCOLATE...
AND HOT DOGS...
AND BUBBLE GUM AND...**COOKIES**
AND POPSICLES AND PEANUT BUTTER AND JELLY.

THEY DECIDED TO GO TO...**THE PARK**

WHEN THEY GOT THERE, THE GREAT BIG DADDY BEAR OPENED THE
DOOR AND ALL OF THE COOKIES FELL OUT OF THE CAR.

THE BABY BEAR SAID "SOMEONE IS IN THIS HOUSE."
THE MAMA BEAR SAID "I BOUGHT THOSE FROOT LOOPS TO EAT MYSELF."
THE GREAT BIG DADDY BEAR SAID...**YOU ALL MAKE TOO MUCH NOISE.**

GOLDILOCKS BEGAN TO CRY...
"I WANT TO LEAVE THE PARK.
I WANT TO GO HOME."

BUT THE CAR HAD A FLAT TIRE AND THEY ALL HAD TO SLEEP THAT
NIGHT IN THE BACK SEAT, AND THE GREAT BIG DADDY BEAR
GRUMBLED "YOU ALL MAKE TOO MUCH NOISE." ALL NIGHT LONG.

*** THE END ***

PRESS "RETURN" PLEASE

Remember the rhyme about the old lady who swallowed a fly?
Here's a variation of that story in PILOT. Notice the use of modules in this repetitive poem.

list
```
R:THE LITTLE OLD LADY AND OTHER POEMS JAS 1973
CH:
T:HELLO, WHAT WOULD YOU LIKE ME TO CALL YOU?
A:$NAME
CH:
T:HELP ME WRITE A POEM, $NAME. HERE WE GO.
T:
T:POOR LITTLE OLD LADY, SHE SWALLOWED A FLY.
U:*S1
R:LINE:09
CA:9,39
A:$AN1
CH:
T:IT SQUIRMED AND WIGGLED AND TICKLED INSIDE HER.
U:*S2
U:*S1
R:LINE:08
CA:8,39
A:$AN2
CH:
T:HOW STRANGE TO SWALLOW A $AN2.
U:*S3
U:*S2
U:*S1
R:LINE:09
```

CA: 9, 39
A: $AN3
CH:
T: THINK OF THAT! SHE SWALLOWED A $AN3.
U: *S4
U: *S3
U: *S2
U: *S1
R: LINE: 10
CA: 10, 39
A: $AN4
CH:
T: SHE LOST HER COOL WHEN SHE SWALLOWED THE $AN4.
U: *S5
U: *S4
U: *S3
U: *S2
U: *S1
R: LINE: 11
CA: 11, 39
A: $AN5
CH:
T: I DON'T KNOW HOW SHE SWALLOWED A $AN5.
T: SHE SWALLOWED THE $AN5 TO CATCH THE $AN4,
U: *S5
U: *S4
U: *S3
U: *S2
T: I DON'T KNOW WHY SHE SWALLOWED THE FLY.
T: POOR LITTLE OLD LADY, I THINK SHE'LL DIE.
T:
PA: 03
T: POOR LITTLE OLD LADY, SHE SWALLOWED A HORSE.
T: SHE DIED, OF COURSE.
PA: 03
R: LINE: 15
R: COL: 30
CA: 15, 30

FOOT:
CH:
T: WOULD YOU LIKE ANOTHER POEM, $NAME?
A:
M: NO
JY: *END
J: ISABEL

*S1
T: I DON'T KNOW WHY SHE SWALLOWED THE FLY.
T: POOR LITTLE OLD LADY, I THINK SHE'LL DIE.
T:
T:
T:
T: POOR LITTLE OLD LADY, SHE SWALLOWED A
R: COL: 39
CA: 1, 39
E:

*S2
T: SHE SWALLOWED THE $AN1 TO CATCH THE FLY.
E:

*S3
T: SHE SWALLOWED THE $AN2 TO CATCH THE $AN1,
E:

*S4
T: SHE SWALLOWED THE $AN3 TO CATCH THE $AN2,
E:

*S5
T: SHE SWALLOWED THE $AN4 TO CATCH THE $AN3,
E:

*ISABEL
CH:
T: SINCE YOU DIDN'T SAY "NO", YOU GET TO READ

```
T: THE ADVENTURES OF ISABEL
T:
T: ISABEL MET AN ENORMOUS
R: LINE: 04
R: COL: 24
CA: 4, 24
A: $AN6
CH:
T: ISABEL, ISABEL, DIDN'T CARE.
T: THE $AN6 WAS HUNGRY, THE $AN6 WAS RAVENOUS,
T: THE $AN6'S BIG MOUTH WAS CRUEL AND CAVERNOUS.
T: THE $AN6 SAID, "ISABEL, GLAD TO MEET YOU,
T: HOW DO, ISABEL, NOW I'LL EAT YOU!"
T: ISABEL, ISABEL, DIDN'T WORRY,
T: ISABEL DIDN'T SCREAM OR SCURRY. SHE
R: LINE: 07
R: COL: 38
CA: 7, 38
A: $AN7
CH:
T: ONCE ON A NIGHT AS BLACK AS PITCH
T: ISABEL MET A WICKED OLD
R: LINE: 02
R: COL: 25
CA: 2, 25
A: $AN8
CH:
T: THE $AN8'S FACE WAS CROSS AND WRINKLED,
T: THE $AN8'S MOUTH WITH TEETH WAS SPRINKLED.
T: HO, HO, ISABEL! THE OLD $AN8 CROWED,
T: I'LL TURN YOU INTO AN UGLY TOAD!
T: ISABEL, ISABEL, DIDN'T WORRY,
T: ISABEL DIDN'T SCREAM OR SCURRY. SHE
T: $AN7 AGAIN.
T:
PA: 10
*END
T: THAT'S ALL FOR NOW, $NAME. TRY SOME POEMS ON YOUR OWN!
```

```
T:                    PRESS "RETURN" NOW
A:
E:
```

RUN
HELLO, WHAT WOULD YOU LIKE ME TO CALL YOU?
SAMMY
HELP ME WRITE A POEM, SAMMY. HERE WE GO.

POOR LITTLE OLD LADY, SHE SWALLOWED A FLY.
I DON'T KNOW WHY SHE SWALLOWED THE FLY.
POOR LITTLE OLD LADY, I THINK SHE'LL DIE.

POOR LITTLE OLD LADY, SHE SWALLOWED A
FROG
IT SQUIRMED AND WIGGLED AND TICKLED INSIDE HER.
SHE SWALLOWED THE FROG TO CATCH THE FLY.
I DON'T KNOW WHY SHE SWALLOWED THE FLY.
POOR LITTLE OLD LADY, I THINK SHE'LL DIE.

POOR LITTLE OLD LADY, SHE SWALLOWED A
BIRD
HOW STRANGE TO SWALLOW A BIRD.
SHE SWALLOWED THE BIRD TO CATCH THE FROG,
SHE SWALLOWED THE FROG TO CATCH THE FLY.
I DON'T KNOW WHY SHE SWALLOWED THE FLY.
POOR LITTLE OLD LADY, I THINK SHE'LL DIE.

POOR LITTLE OLD LADY, SHE SWALLOWED A
CAT
THINK OF THAT! SHE SWALLOWED A CAT.
SHE SWALLOWED THE CAT TO CATCH THE BIRD,
SHE SWALLOWED THE BIRD TO CATCH THE FROG,
SHE SWALLOWED THE FROG TO CATCH THE FLY.
I DON'T KNOW WHY SHE SWALLOWED THE FLY.
POOR LITTLE OLD LADY, I THINK SHE'LL DIE.

POOR LITTLE OLD LADY, SHE SWALLOWED A
DOG
SHE LOST HER COOL WHEN SHE SWALLOWED THE DOG.
SHE SWALLOWED THE DOG TO CATCH THE CAT,
SHE SWALLOWED THE CAT TO CATCH THE BIRD,
SHE SWALLOWED THE BIRD TO CATCH THE FROG,
SHE SWALLOWED THE FROG TO CATCH THE FLY.
I DON'T KNOW WHY SHE SWALLOWED THE FLY.
POOR LITTLE OLD LADY, I THINK SHE'LL DIE.

POOR LITTLE OLD LADY, SHE SWALLOWED A
COW
I DON'T KNOW HOW SHE SWALLOWED A COW.
SHE SWALLOWED THE COW TO CATCH THE DOG,
SHE SWALLOWED THE DOG TO CATCH THE CAT,
SHE SWALLOWED THE CAT TO CATCH THE BIRD,
SHE SWALLOWED THE BIRD TO CATCH THE FROG,
SHE SWALLOWED THE FROG TO CATCH THE FLY.
I DON'T KNOW WHY SHE SWALLOWED THE FLY.
POOR LITTLE OLD LADY, I THINK SHE'LL DIE.

POOR LITTLE OLD LADY, SHE SWALLOWED A HORSE.
SHE DIED, OF COURSE.
Press "RETURN" to go on

WOULD YOU LIKE ANOTHER POEM, SAMMY?
SURE
SINCE YOU DIDN'T SAY "NO," YOU GET TO READ
THE ADVENTURES OF ISABEL

ISABEL MET AN ENORMOUS
FIERCE GIANT
ISABEL, ISABEL, DIDN'T CARE.
THE FIERCE GIANT WAS HUNGRY, THE FIERCE GIANT WAS RAVENOUS,
THE FIERCE GIANT'S BIG MOUTH WAS CRUEL AND CAVERNOUS.
THE FIERCE GIANT SAID, "ISABEL, GLAD TO MEET YOU,
HOW DO, ISABEL, NOW I'LL EAT YOU!"
ISABEL, ISABEL, DIDN'T WORRY,

ISABEL DIDN'T SCREAM OR SCURRY. SHE
RAN AND RAN IN A HURRY

ONCE ON A NIGHT AS BLACK AS PITCH
ISABEL MET A WICKED OLD
WITCH
THE WITCH'S FACE WAS CROSS AND WRINKLED,
THE WITCH'S MOUTH WITH TEETH WAS SPRINKLED.
HO, HO, ISABEL! THE OLD WITCH CROWED,
I'LL TURN YOU INTO AN UGLY TOAD!
ISABEL, ISABEL, DIDN'T WORRY,
ISABEL DIDN'T SCREAM OR SCURRY. SHE
RAN AND RAN IN A HURRY AGAIN.

THAT'S ALL FOR NOW, SAMMY. TRY SOME POEMS ON YOUR OWN!
PRESS "RETURN" NOW

FILE COMMANDS

For more serious purposes, PILOT has been used to collect research data that can be analyzed by other programs. In order to collect the information in a file, one must have a means to create and open a file and then write information into it, either identifying information from the program or information gathered from the user of the program. In one version of PILOT, the statements used are:

CREATEF:	to create a file so its name is known to the system.
OPENF:	to open a file for the collection of data.
WRITE: (or WR:)	to write an entry into the file.
RW:	to write text from the RW: statement into the file.
EOF:	to write an end-of-file mark into the file.
CLOSEF:	to close the file after use.

These statement types and other related instructions for file manipulation will not be explained here, but they are an important element in using PILOT for data collection. You will find descriptions of these statement types accompanied by examples in the programmer's reference manual for your version of PILOT.

The following is an example showing the collection of responses to a questionnaire such as one that might be used in market research.

list
```
R: QUESTON.PLT collects information about Brand Z in ZDATA.
openf:x,zdata
    r: A file called zdata is opened and will be referred to
    r: by a number stored in variable x.
t:Have you ever seen or heard of Brand Z products? Yes..1 No..2
a:#a
wr:x
    r: The response is stored in #a and written to the file.
  m: 2
  jy: *QUIT


*q18b
T:Have Brand Z products EVER BEEN used in your home? Yes..1 No..2
a:
wr:x
  m: 2
  jy: *QUIT


*q18c
T:WHEN did you LAST use Brand Z?
a:
wr:x
T:WHICH of the Brand Z products have been used? (enter up to 5)
    r: Here we collect a list of potential topics.
a:$types
wr:x
m:filling
jn:*pieces
    r: the rw: statement writes a remark to the file.
rw:x,filling
```

```
t: How often have you BOUGHT Brand Z filling?
a:
wr: x
t: What do you like about Brand Z filling?
a:
wr: x
      r: Other questions about filling can be asked here.
*pieces
      r: put the list of types back into the entry buffer
a: =$types
m: pieces
jn: *sauce
rw: x, pieces
t: How often have you BOUGHT Brand Z pieces?
a:
wr: x


*sauce
a: =$types
m: sauce
jn: *tomatoes
rw: x, sauce
t: How often have you BOUGHT Brand Z sauce?
a:
wr: x


*tomatoes
a: =$types
m: tomatoes
jn: *dinners
rw: x, tomatoes
t: How often have you BOUGHT Brand Z canned tomatoes?
a:
wr: x


*dinners
a: =$types
```

143

```
m: dinners
jn: *other
rw: x, dinners
t: How often have you BOUGHT Brand Z frozen dinners?
a:
wr: x


*other
t: How often have you BOUGHT Brand Z "other" items?
a:
wr: x

*QUIT
     r: The file is closed after writing an end-of-file mark.
closef: x
load: analysis
```

run

Have you ever seen or heard of Brand Z products? Yes..1 No..2
1
Have Brand Z products EVER BEEN used in your home? Yes..1 No..2
1
WHEN did you LAST use Brand Z?
about 2 weeks ago
WHICH of the Brand Z products have been used? (enter up to 5)
filling, frozen dinners
How often have you BOUGHT Brand Z filling?
2 or 3 times
What do you like about Brand Z filling?
It's very smooth
How often have you BOUGHT Brand Z frozen dinners?
only 1 time
How often have you BOUGHT Brand Z "other" items?
not at all
This line is displayed by the analysis program that has not been completed.

LINKAGE TO OTHER PROGRAMS

The example just shown also demonstrates one method of linkage to another program in the final statement "load:analysis". In this case, "analysis" is another PILOT program that is to be loaded from disk storage and put into operation, perhaps to analyze the data gathered in the file called "zdata", which was just created.

A more likely case would be that a program for the analysis of such data gathered for many respondents might have been written in FORTRAN, COBOL, or another language more suited for arithmetic or statistics than PILOT. For this purpose, PILOT uses the statement XS: which stands for EXecute System. The text following the colon in an XS: statement becomes a command line for the operating system. It can therefore cause operation of an external existing program that is not a PILOT program.

SCREEN-ORIENTED DATA COLLECTION

The following is a portion of a more complex program used to collect bibliographic information. It first presents a menu of four choices: 1. to add information about an article in a journal; 2. to add information about a book or a chapter in a book; 3. to create a memo note or describe an unclassified item of information; or 4. to quit the entire operation. Each of the first three choices results in a display making use of a 24- by-80-character screen and fields for the entry of information at specific locations on the screen. Indication of where information is to be entered is dependent on the program's ability to control both the placement of presented information and the cursor.

```
list
r:              BIB.PLT Collects bibliography information
*initia

r: prefill strings. These dotted lines are used to indicate entry
areas.
c: $D7=...................................................................
```

```
c: $D6=. . . . . . . . . . . . . . . . . . . . . . . . . . . . . . . . . . . . . . . . . . . . . . . . . . . . . . . . . . . . . . . . . . . . . . . . .
c: $D2=. . . . . . . . . . . . . . . . . . . .
c: g=0
c: i=0


r: open the file for citations
     ch:
t:
t: Enter the name of the collection file to be used (e.g. b:bib.doc)
     a: $filename
r:  openf:$filename,z This will later be used to open a data file
r:  append:z          and new data will be added to earlier data.


*go r: This is an initial selection menu with four choices.
     ch:
t:
t: UCSF Shared Bibliography Entry System     Draft Version
t:
t: Add items to the temporary list
t:  a-Article in a journal
t:  b-Book or chapter in a book
t:  m-Memo or other unclassified item
t:
t:  q-quit
t:



*reask
th: Your choice? (pick a letter):
     a:
     m: a
     jy: addart
     m: b
     jy: addboo
     m: m
     jy: addmem
     m: q
     jy: quit
     j: reask
```

146

```
r:Accept input to $temp. Y-switch = null input.
*ntr
    ah: $temp
    c: $fake=>$temp<
    a: =$fake
    m: ><
    e:
*fill70
r:  fill 70 char line with dots
    ca: r, c
    t: $d7
    ca: r, c
    e:


*fill60
r:  fill 60 char line with dots
    ca: r, c
    t: $d6
    ca: r, c
    e:


*fill20
r:  fill 20 char line with dots
    ca: r, c
    t: $d2
    ca: r, c
    e:


r:  Enter up to 12 authors
*au_entry
    c: n=0
    c: r=2
    c: c=61
*au_more
    c: n=n+1
    e(n-12):
    c: c=c+24
r:  If new line
    c(c-60): r=r+1
```

```
                c (c-60) : c=12
                ca: r, c
                u: fill20
    r:  Construct the a: statement
                u: ntr
                cl:
                jy: au_end
                c: $entry=c: $au#n=$temp
    r:  Now use it
                xi: $entry
                j: au_more
   *au_end
                c: $entry=c: $au#n=^
                xi: $entry
                e:
    r:  Fix (reedit) up to 12 authors
                *au_fix
                c: n=0
                c: r=2
                c: c=61
   *af_more
                c: n=n+1
                c: $entry=ah: =$au#n
                xi: $entry
                m: ^
                ey:
                e (n-12) :
                c: c=c+24
    r:  If new line
                c (c-60) : r=r+1
                c (c-60) : c=12
                ca: r, c
                u: ntr
                jy: af_more
                c: $entry=c: $au#n=$temp
                xi: $entry
                j: af_more
```

```
*addart
   c: g=g+1
   ch:
t: Adding an article. Now adding number #g.
t:
t: Author(s):
t:            (for example, Jones RB)
t:
t:
t:
t: Journal (abbrev.):
t: Year:      Vol:      Pages:
t:
t: Title:
t:
t:
t:
t:
t: Notes:
t:
t:
t:
t:
t:
t:
t:
th: a- Article b- Book m- Mem of- Fix q- Quit Your choice:


u: au_entry


*journ
   c: r=8
   c: c=20
   u: fill60
   ah: $jo
   cl:
```

```
        ca: 9, 8
        ah: $yr
        ca: 9, 32
        ah: $vo
        ca: 9, 56
        ah: $pg

        c: r=10
        c: c=8
        c: n=0
*ti_more
        c: r=r+1
        c: n=n+1
        j (r-14) : ti_end
        u: fill70
        u: ntr
        cl:
        jy: ti_end
        c: $entry=c: $ti#n=$temp
        xi: $entry
        j: ti_more
*ti_end
        c: $entry=c: $ti#n=
        xi: $entry
*notes
        c: r=15
        c: n=0
*no_more
        c: r=r+1
        c: n=n+1
        j (r-23) : no_end
        c: c=8
        u: fill70
        u: ntr
        cl:
        jy: no_end
        c: $entry=c: $no#n=$temp
        xi: $entry
```

150

```
        j: no_more
    *no_end
        c: $entry=c: $no#n=ˆ
        xi: $entry


    *choose
        ca: 24, 67
        cl:
        inmax: 1
        ah: $choice
        inmax: 80
        m: f, F
        jy: fix
    r:  write output record here
        u: artout
        a: =$choice
        m: a, A
        jy: addart
        m: b, B
        jy: addboo
        m: m, M
        jy: addmem
        j: go

        r: *********

*fix
r:  Image is on screen. Place cursor and retrieve $variables for changes.
r:  CR goes to next field.

u: au_fix


*jof
    ca: 8, 20
    u: ntr
    jy: yrf
    c: $jo=$temp
```

```
*yrf
    ca: 9, 8
    u: ntr
    jy: vof
    c: $yr=$temp


*vof
    ca: 9, 32
    u: ntr
    jy: pgf
    c: $vo=$temp


*pgf
    ca: 9, 56
    u: ntr
    jy: tif
    c: $pg=$temp


*tif
    c: r=10
    c: c=8
    c: n=0
*tif_more
    c: r=r+1
    c: n=n+1
    j(r-15): notesf
    c: $entry=ah: =$ti#n
    xi: $entry
    m: ^
    jy: notesf
    ca: r, c
    u: ntr
    jy: tif_more
    c: $entry=c: $ti#n=$temp
    xi: $entry
j: tif_more
```

152

```
*notesf
    c:r=15
    c:n=0
*nof_more
    c:r=r+1
    c:n=n+1
    j(r-22):choose
c:$entry=ah:=$no#n
    xi:$entry
    m:^
    jy:*choose
    ca:r,c
    u:ntr
    jy:nof_more
    c:$entry=c:$no#n=$temp
    xi:$entry
    j:nof_more


*addboo
    c:g=g+1
    ch:
t:Adding a book or chapter. Now adding number #g.
t:
t:Author(s):
t:              (for example, Jones RB)
t:
t:
t:
t:Chapter:
t:
t:Book:
t:
t:Section
t:Year:          Edition:
t:Volume:        Pages:
t:Editor(s):
t:
```

```
t: Publisher:        Place:
t:
t: Notes:
t:
t:
t:
t:
th: a- Article b- Book m- Memo f- Fix q- Quit Your choice:

    u: au_entry
*book
    c: r=8
    c: c=10
    u: fill70
    u: ntr
    cl:
        cy: $chap1=^
        jy: booknm
    c: $chap1=$temp
    cl:
    c: r=9
    u: fill70
    ah: $chap2
    cl:


*booknm
    c: r=10
    u: fill70
    ah: $bo1
    cl:
    c: r=11
    u: fill70
    ah: $bo2
    cl:

    c: r=12
    u: fill70
    ah: $sect
    cl:
```

154

```
            ca: 13, 10
            ah: $yr

            ca: 13, 36
            ah: $edn

    ca: 14, 10
            ah: $vo

            ca: 14, 36
            ah: $pg

            c: n=0
            c: r=15
            c: c=12
*ed_more
            c: n=n+1
            j (n-3) : ed_end
            u: fill20
            u: ntr
            cl:
            jy: ed_end
            c: $entry=c: $ed#n=$temp
            xi: $entry
            c: c=c+24
            j: ed_more
*ed_end
            c: $entry=c: $ed#n=^
            xi: $entry


*bpub
            ca: 17, 12
            ah: $pub

            ca: 17, 36
            ah: $p1

            c: r=18
            c: n=0
```

155

```
*bno_more
    c: r=r+1
    c: n=n+1
    j (r-23): bno_end
    c: c=8
    u: fill70
    u: ntr
    cl:
    jy: bno_end
    c: $entry=c: $no#n=$temp
    xi: $entry
    j: bno_more
*bno_end
    c: $entry=c: $no#n=^
    xi: $entry


*bchoose
    ca: 24, 67
    cl:
    inmax: 1
    ah: $choice
    inmax: 80
    m: f, F
    jy: bfix
r: write output record here
    u: bookout
    a: =$choice
    m: a, A
    jy: addart
    m: b, B
    jy: addboo
    m: m, M
    jy: addmem
    j: go


*bfix
r: Image is on screen. Place cursor and retrieve $variables for changes.
```

```
r: CR goes to next field.

    u: au_fix
*chf
    ca: 8, 10
    u: ntr
    jy: bof
    c: $chap1=$temp
    ca: 9, 10
    u: ntr
    jy: bof
    c: $chap2=$temp

*bof
    ca: 10, 10
    u: ntr
    jy: sef
    c: $bol=$temp
    ca: 11, 10
    j: ntr
    jysef
    c: $bo2=$temp

*sef
    ca: 12, 10
    u: ntr
    jy: byrf
    c: $sect=$temp

*byrf
    ca: 13, 10
    u: ntr
    jy: editf
    c: $yr=$temp

*editf
    ca: 13, 36
    u: ntr
```

```
    jy: bvof
    c: $edit=$temp


*bvof
    ca: 14, 10
    u: ntr
    jy: bpgf
    c: $vo=$temp


*bpgf
    ca: 14, 36
    u: ntr
    jy: edf
    c: $pg=$temp


*edf
    c: n=0
    c: r=15
    c: c=12
*edf_more
    c: n=n+1
    j (n-3) : pubf
    c: $entry=ah: =$ef#n
    xi: $entry
    m: ^
    jy: pubf
    ca: r, c
    u: ntr
    c: c=c+24
    jy: edf_more
    c: $entry=c: $ed#n=$temp
    xi: $entry
    j: edf_more


*pubf
    ca: 17, 12
    u: ntr
    jy: plf
    c: $pub=$temp
```

```
*plf
   ca: 17, 36
   u: ntr
   jy: bnof
   c: $pl=$temp


*bnof
   c: r=18
   c: c=8
   c: n=0
*bnof2
   c: r=r+1
   c: n=n+1
   j (r-23): bchoose
   c: $entry=ah: =$no#n
   xi: $entry
   m: ^
   jy: bchoose
   ca: r, c
   u: ntr
jy: bnof2
   c: $entry=c: $no#n=$temp
   xi: $entry
   j: bnof2


r: **********************************


*addmem
   c: g=g+1
   ch:
t: Adding a memo.  Now adding number #g.
t:
t: Author (s):
t:                (e.g.  Jones RB)
t:
t: Journal (abbrev.):  MEMO
t: Date:                    Vol: 1           Pages: 1-1
t:
t: Title:
```

```
t:
t:Notes:
t:
t:
t:
t:
t:
t:
t:
t:
t:
t:
t:
t:
th:a- Article b- Book m- Memo f- Fix q- Quit Your choice:

    u:au_entry
    c:$jo=MEMO

    ca:7,8
    ah:$yr

    c:$vo=1
    c:$pg=1-1

    c:r=9
    c:c=8
    u:fill70
    ah:$ti
    cl:

*memo
    c:n=0
    c:r=10
*memo2
    c:r=r+1
    c:n=n+1
    j(r-23):memo_end
```

160

```
    u:fill70
    u:ntr
    cl:
    jy:memo_end
    c:$entry=c:$no#n=$temp
    xi:$entry
    j:memo2
*memo_end
    c:$entry=c:$no#n=^
    xi:$entry


*mchoose
    ca:24,67
    cl:
    inmax:1
    ah:$choice
    inmax:80
    m:f,F
    jy:mfix


r:write output record here
    u:memout
    a:=$choice
    m:a,A
    jy:addart
    m:b,B
    jy:addboo
    m:m,M
    jy:addmem
    j:go


*mfix
    u:au_fix
    ca:7,8
    u:ntr
    jy:mtf
    c:$yr=$temp
```

```
*mtf
    ca: 9, 8
    u: ntr
    jy: memof
    c: $ti=$temp

*memof
    c: r=10
    c: n=0
*memf2
    c: r=r+1
    c: n=n+1
    c: c=8
    j (r-23): mchoose
    c: $entry=ah: =$no#n
    xi: $entry
    m: ^
    jy: mchoose
    ca: r, c
    u: ntr
    jy: memf2
    c: $entry=c: $no#n=$temp
    xi: $entry
    j: memf2
        r: Here is where the collected $variables will be written
        r: into the file in a proper format.
*artout
    e:
*bookout
    e:
*memout
    e:

*quit
    closef: z
    e:
```

This example makes a great deal of use of modules for functions
that are repetitive; it uses some advanced functions that may not

be present in all versions of PILOT. Even within the same version of PILOT, there are certainly many equivalent ways to have PILOT present the same information and gather the same data. If you study what has been done here, you may find new methods that you can use in your own application. For example, string variables can be used to display the same thing in different locations on the screen.

The display makes use of data entry areas on the display screen that are defined by dotted lines. At the beginning of the program, C: statements are used to define string variables used for this purpose. At a point in the program where we wish to place a line of twenty dots, for instance, we determine the position by setting the values of r (for row position) and c (for column position), and then call the module *fill20 that contains a T: statement making reference to the string $d2. This occurs for each place where we wish to allow the entry of another author's name. The values of r and c are calculated in order to allow three authors' names on each line, up to four lines.

After defining these string variables and making sure that the numeric variables g and i (used for counting) begin at zero, the program allows entry of a file name and then presents a menu of choices, allowing data collection in three different formats. It is easy to see what will be shown on the display screen by looking at the array of T: statements to see what section of the program will then become active in response to each allowable choice. Since people don't always follow directions, programs like this should be designed to respond reasonably to any input. In this case, an unexpected response simply causes the question to be asked again.

Taking the first branch of the menu to *addart, you will see the display defined by T: statements followed by the use of module *au_entry, where authors' names are collected. The special TH: form of the T: statement and the AH: form of the A: statement are used in some cases to prevent the cursor's moving to a new line. Except for the final location of the cursor, the TH: statement is the same as the T: statement, and the AH: statement is the same as the A: statement. Within the *au_entry module, values of "r" and "c" are calculated in order to place the next entry in the proper screen location, and the *fill20 module is used to put a row of dots there.

The next section of the *au_entry module uses some advanced features in order to recognize a null entry (pressing RE-

TURN without other input) as a signal to stop entering names. Look at the module named *ntr to see how this is done. Since most versions of PILOT don't have a function for determining the length of a string, we must be inventive within the functions it *does* have. An AH: statement (A: without starting a new line) is used to accept input to $temp. The string $temp is then surrounded by the arbitrary characters ">" and "<" and the result (in $fake) is moved into the accept buffer to test for a match with "><". If there is a match, then we know that the string $temp is empty, indicating a null entry as described above. If there is not a match with "><", the entry can be retrieved from $temp.

Successive authors' names are stored using numbered string variable names such as "$au1", "$au2", and so on. This is accomplished by using a C: statement to create such names as needed as part of another C: statement placed in a variable called $entry. The XI: statement (execute immediate) causes PILOT to interpret the contents of $entry as a PILOT statement and act upon it. For example, when the value of n is 1, $entry is caused to contain "C:$au1=$temp" and XI:$entry then causes PILOT to use that statement, putting the original authors' name (earlier put in $temp) into $au1. Similar methods are used in collecting information for books, chapters within books, and memos.

To complete the program, the dummy modules named *artout, *bookout, and *memout need to contain statements to write the contents of appropriate variables (such as $au1, $au2, and so on) into a data collection file in a format appropriate for later retrieval or printing.

164

Quizzes and Examinations

GUESSING A NUMBER
CHOSEN BY THE PROGRAM

The same functions of presenting information and collecting answers are what is needed for giving a quiz or examination. The general principles can be shown in a simple guessing game in which the computer uses a random number function to choose a number between 1 and one 100, and the subject is prompted to find the number with as few guesses as possible.

list
```
R:  GUESS A NUMBER BETWEEN 1 AND 100

CH:
    R: We will use N for the number to be guessed,
    R:             T for the number of guesses (tries), and
    R:             G for the guess.
*START
C: N=RND(100)
C: T=0
T:
T: THE COMPUTER HAS CHOSEN A NUMBER BETWEEN 1 AND 100.
T: TRY TO GUESS WHAT IT IS WITH AS FEW TRIES AS POSSIBLE.
T: THE COMPUTER WILL TELL YOU IF YOU ARE HIGH, LOW, OR CORRECT.
T:
```

```
*NEXT
T: GO AHEAD AND ENTER YOUR GUESS, THEN PRESS "RETURN".
A: #G
C: T=T+1
J (G=N) : RIGHT
T (G>N) : YOUR GUESS IS TOO HIGH, GUESS AGAIN.
J (G>N) : *NEXT
T: YOUR GUESS IS TOO LOW, GUESS AGAIN.
J: *NEXT

*RIGHT
T: CONGRATULATIONS!
T (T=1) : WOW! YOU GUESSED IT ON THE FIRST TRY.
T (T<>1) : YOU GUESSED IT IN #T TRIES.
T (T>7) : THERE IS A WAY TO ALWAYS DO BETTER THAN THAT.
T:
T: DO YOU WANT TO TRY AGAIN?
A:
M: Y
TY: OK, THE COMPUTER IS CHOOSING.
PAY: 5
JY: START
TN: OK, THANKS FOR PLAYING. GOODBYE.
E:
```

The program just shown starts by clearing the display screen and then initializing the values of N (an unpredictable number between 1 and 100) and T (starting at zero to represent the number of guesses). After giving introductory directions, guesses are accepted until the value entered (stored in G) matches the value of N. After the correct guess is made, an appropriate comment is made, depending on how many guesses were made. By providing a special comment for a lucky first-try success, you can avoid an ungrammatical "You guessed it in 1 tries."

By making each guess divide the remaining possible numbers into equal groups (a method called *binary search*), the user will be able to discover the number between 1 and 100 with a maximum of seven guesses. (A comment has been provided for cases where an unreasonably large number of guesses was made.)

TESTING FOR SPECIFIC KNOWLEDGE

The close relationship between teaching, testing, and data gathering can be seen in a program that tests a diabetic patient's knowledge of management methods and collects data about the extent of the patient's knowledge while being instructive. The program content was developed by Peggy Huang, R.N., and Hyo Kim, M.D. This is, of course, presented here as an example of programming in PILOT and not as a source of authoritative medical informatipon.

```
list
R: Diabetes information from patients.
R: Peggy Huang, RN; Hyo Kim, MD; J. Starkweather, Ph.D.
CH:
OPENF: PATIENT, P
APPEND: P
T:  Before we start, I would like to know a little bit about you
:What is your first name, please?
A: $fname
WRITE: P
t: I will call you $fname, ok?
t:
:And your last name?
a: $lname
WRITE: P
t:
:How old are you?
a: #A
RW: P, AGE=#A YRS OLD.
    r: The RW: command is an R: statement written to a file.
    r: In this case, the file reference is P.
t:
:How many years have you had diabetes?
a: #B
RW: P, DIABETIC FOR #B YRS.
    r: #Q is number of questions to be asked.
    r: 22 questions are asked those who take insulin.
    r: 13 questions if they do not take insulin.
c: Q=22
```

```
ch:
t:Do you take insulin?
a:  $insulin
m:  y, pos, right, correct
cy: I=1
    r:Non-zero value for I means insulin.
cn:  Q=13
uy: insulin
t:Do you take an oral diabetic medication?
a:
m:  y, pos, right, correct
uy: oral



ch:
t:It would help me to know how much you understand about
:diabetes. I will ask you #Q multiple choice questions.
:I would like you to pick the choice that seems most correct.
:This will take approximately 30 minutes.
:Relax and take your time. If you have any questions,
:don't hesitate to ask a staff member.
:Here we go.
    r:S = score
c:S=0
foot:
ch:
C:n=0
t:1. Diabetes means
t:
:       1) improper eating habits
:       2) inability of the body to get rid of excess sugar
:       3) too little energy from food
:       4) too much energy from food
u:check
m:2
ty:correct.
cy:S=S+1
tn:Not quite. 2 is the correct answer.
foot:
```

ch:

t: 2. Blood sugar is too high in uncontrolled diabetes because

t:

:   1) the body does not produce enough insulin

:   2) the insulin produced by the body cannot work properly

:   3) both 1) and 2)

:   4) none of the above

u: check

m: 3

ty: Right.

cy: S=S+1

tn: No, both 1 and 2 are right.

tn: The correct answer would be 3.

foot:

ch:

t: 3. Insulin

t:

:   1) raises blood sugar.

:   2) makes sugar available for the body.

:   3) causes fat to disappear.

:   4) makes sugars from proteins and fats.

u: check

m: 2

ty: O. K.

cy: S=S+1

tn: 2 is the correct answer.

foot:

ch:

t: 4. Diabetics

t:

:   1) must have between-meal snacks.

:   2) should avoid all active sports or strenuous activities.

:   3) should be aware of changes in the environment.

:   which can upset the control of diabetes.

:   4) should avoid traveling.

u: check

m: 3
ty: Right on!
cy: S=S+1
tn: No, 3 would be the best answer.
foot:

ch:
t: 5. The oral hypoglycemic agents (diabetic pills)
t:
:   1) are a form of oral insulin.
:   2) can be given only if the pancreas can
              still produce insulin.
:   3) are given to reduce weight.
:   4) are often given with insulin.
u: check
m: 2
ty: Good.
cy: S=S+1
tn: Sorry, 2 is right.
foot:

ch:
t: 6. The signs and symptoms of hypoglycemia (high blood sugar)
:   are
:
:   1) excessive thirst and urination.
:   2) sudden onset of shakiness.
:   3) cold sweat.
:   4) all of the above.
u: check
m: 1
ty: Yes, yes.
tn: The only right answer is 1.
cy: S=S+1
tn: The sudden onset of shakiness or a cold sweat are
tn: signs of HYPOglycemia.
foot:

ch:

t: 7. Ketoacidosis is caused by insulin deficiency.

:   This can be due to

t:

:   1) infection.

:   2) heart attack.

:   3) not taking enough insulin.

:   4) all of the above.

u: check

m: 4

ty: Correct!

cy: S=S=1

tn: All are right.

foot:

ch:

t: 8. The symptoms of ketoacidosis (diabetic acidosis) are

t:

:   1) nervousness.

:   2) nausea and vomiting.

:   3) both 1) and 2).

:   4) none of the above.

u: check

m: 2

ty: Right.

cy: S=S+1

tn: No, 2 is right answer.

foot:

ch:

t: 9. Possible diabetic ketoacidosis may be suspected

:   at home by

:

:   1) 4+ (2%) urine sugar test.

:   2) negative urine sugar and strongly positive
              urine ketone test.

:   3) 4+ (2%) urine sugar and strongly positive ketone test.

172

:   4) sudden loss of consciousness.
u: check
m: 3
y: Very good!
n: No, a urine test usually shows strongly positive
n: for both sugar and ketone.
foot:

ch:
t: 10. Diabetics can prevent foot problems by
t:
:   1) frequent cleaning of feet in hot water.
:   2) cutting extra skin off calluses nightly.
:   3) barefoot exercises on wooden floor.
:   4) none of the above.
u: check
m: 4
ty: Very good.
cy: S=S+1
tn: No, all of them may cause foot ulcers.
foot:

ch:
t: 11. If you have a cut on your foot
t:
:   1) immediately apply iodine to prevent infection.
:   2) keep the foot clean with soap and water and see your
:   doctor if the cut does not heal quickly.
:   3) both 1) and 2).
:   4) neither 1) nor 2).
u: check
m: 3
ty: Right!
cy: S=S+1
tn: No, both are correct.
foot:

```
ch:
t:12. A diabetic diet is
t:
:     1) a diet that limits carbohydrates only.
:     2) a measured food plan that can never change.
:     3) a well-balanced diet that the whole family may use.
:     4) a plan requiring many special foods.
u: check
m: 3
ty: excellent!
cy:  S=S+1
tn: Not really, 3 is right.
foot:


ch:
t:  13. Limiting foods that have large amounts of saturated
:        fats and cholesterol is
:
:     1) to reduce the risk of developing heart disease.
:     2) only important if the patient is overweight.
:     3) not important in a diabetic's diet.
:     4) causes important nutritional deficiencies.
u: check
m: 1
ty: A very good choice
cy:  S= S+1
tn:  1 is correct.
foot:


ch:
u(I): *pr-insulin
t:Your score is #S out of #N.
RW: P, Score= #S/#N
t: Thank you for your cooperation.
t: Take care and good-bye for now.
ca: 8, 26
```

t: ~E N D~
eof:P
closef:P
e:

*pr-insulin:
t:14. Fast-acting insulin
t:
:   1) is NPH or Lente insulin.
:   2) can last 6 to 8 hours in the body.
:   3) lasts up to 24 hours in the body.
:   4) none of the above.
u:check
m: 2
cy:S=S+1
y:True.
n:2 is correct.
foot:

ch:
t:15. You are taking a mixture of NPH 20 units and regular 10
:   units before breakfast every morning.
:   Your urine tests show the following fairly consistently:
t:
t: Before breakfast ....Negative
t: Before lunch ....4+ or 2%
t: Before dinner ....Trace or ¼ %
t: Bedtime ....Negative
t:
t:This means you need
:   1) less insulin.
:   2) more NPH insulin.
:   3) more regular insulin.
:   4) more of both NPH and regular insulin.
u:check
m: 3

y: Very good!
cy: S=S+1
m: 1
y: No, taking less insulin will cause even higher blood sugar
y: and more spillage in the afternoon.
m: 2, 4
y: No, taking more NPH insulin will cause the blood sugar
y: to come down at night time and possibly cause a HYPOglycemic
y: reaction.
foot:
ch:
t: 16. You are getting a total of 40 units of NPH insulin
:   before breakfast.
:
: Your urine test shows:
t: Before breakfast .... Negative
t: Before lunch .... 4+ or 2%
t: Before dinner .... 1+ or ½ %
t: Bedtime .... 2+ or ¾ %
t:
: This means you need
:
:   1) more NPH insulin.
:   2) to change to Lente insulin.
:   3) a mixture of regular and NPH insulin.
:   4) Regular insulin instead of NPH.
u: check
m: 3
cy: S=S+1
y: Excellent! You need to bring down the afternoon sugar
y: with a short-acting insulin.
m: 4
y: Right idea, but you also need an intermediate acting
y: insulin like Lente or NPH to keep the night sugar down.
m: 1
y: No, NPH or Lente insulin peak too late to control
y: high afternoon sugar.
m: 2

y: No, basically, Lente and NPH insulin peak at the
y: same time. You need a short-acting insulin
y: to control the high afternoon sugar.
foot:

ch:
t: 17. You feel that an insulin reaction is coming on.
:   You should first
:
:   1) call your doctor.
:   2) eat some food containing sugar.
:   3) go lie down to see whether the feeling passes.
:   4) test your urine.
u: check
m: 2
cy: S=S+1
y: Right.
n: The most important thing in this situation is
n: to prevent a hypoglycemic reaction by taking
n: some sugar first. The right choice, therefore,
n: is 2.
foot:

ch:
t: 18. Insulin reactions are likely to occur
:
:   1) during vigorous exercises.
:   2) in the middle of night.
:   3) just before lunch or dinner.
:   4) any of the above.
u: check
m: 4
y: Yes, quite true.
cy: S=S+1
n: Right, but insulin reactions may happen during other times
: mentioned above.
foot:

ch:

t: 19. You are on insulin but have the "flu" and are
: unable to eat breakfast. You should
:
:   1) omit insulin entirely.
:   2) take less insulin with negative urine sugar test.
:   3) take more insulin with positive urine sugar test.
:   4) both 2 and 3.
u: check
m: 4
y: correct.
cy: S=S+1
m: 1
y: Wrong. Remember, lack of insulin causes ketoacidosis.
m: 2, 3
y: both 2 and 3 are right, but be sure to take some replacement
y: carbohydrate, like Coke or 7-UP.
foot:

ch:

t: 20. When you are under physical stress (like cold)
:   or a great deal of emotional stress, you will most
:   likely require
:
:   1) more insulin.
:   2) same amount of insulin.
:   3) less insulin.
:   4) no insulin.
u: check
m: 1
y: Yes,
CY: S=S+1
n: No, you need more insulin
t: because during stress, the body produces more
: glucose (gluconeogenesis).
foot:

178

ch:

t: 21. The action of Lente or NPH insulin lasts

:

:   1) about 6 hours.

:   2) about 12 hours.

:   3) about 24 hours.

:   4) about 36 hours.

u: check

m: 3

y: correct.

CY: S=S+1

n: No, it lasts about 24 hours.

foot:

ch:

t: 22. You took 15 units of regular insulin and

:   15 units of NPH (or Lente) insulin before breakfast.

:   You had an insulin reaction before dinner

:   even though you had had a mid-afternoon snack.

:   The reaction is probably due to too much of

:

:   1) regular insulin.

:   2) NPH insulin.

:   3) none of above.

u: check

m: 2

y: Right.

cy: S=S+1

n: No, NPH insulin.

foot.

ch:

    r: end of questions for insulin takers.

e:

*insulin:

t: How many units of NPH or Lente insulin?

```
a: #L
RW: P, TAKES #L UNITS OF NPH (LENTE)  INSULIN.
t: How many units of regular insulin?
a:  #R
RW: P, TAKES #R UNITS of REGULAR  INSULIN.
e:
*oral:
t: Which oral agent do you take?
a: $agent
RW: P, Takes $agent pills.
e:

*check
    r:  Stores answers from 4-choice questions.
    r:  Enter with #Z containing the subject's answer choice.
C: N=N+1
*ch2
t:
a: #Z
m: 1 , 2 , 3 , 4
tn: please answer 1, 2, 3, or 4.
jn: ch2
RW: P, Q. #N= #Z
e:
foot:
```

Although it does provide some information along the way, the program's primary purpose is to gather information about the present state of knowledge of diabetic patients. More questions are asked of those patients who are involved in the management of self-administered insulin. A multiple-choice format is used throughout, with as many of the repetitive elements of data entry as possible put into a module called *check. At each question in the main sequence, a question is posed with four alternative answers, the answer is accepted into the numeric variable #Z, and *check is called. The module increments the count of answers, insists on answers between 1 and 4, and writes the answer into a data collection file. After returning to the main program, different answers cause different comments to be made before the screen is cleared for another question. A standard format is useful when group data is being collected.

REPORTING RESULTS, AND CONVERSION
OF TYPES OF DATA

Particularly in the presentation of results, it is sometimes necessary to convert information stored in a character string variable for use as a numeric quantity, or to convert the contents of a numeric variable to a character string. Computer programming languages often have specific functions for such conversions, but many versions of PILOT do not; the C: statement will usually accomplish what is needed in a natural manner.

For example, the following program segment demonstrates conversion from a string variable to a numeric variable.

```
list
t: Type a number
a: $string
c: n=$string
    r: A "#" is optional, so it could be "c:#n=$string"
t: n= #n
```

In this case, the answer is accepted as a string variable, so there is no automatic check on whether or not numbers in the acceptable range are entered. However, if the input is not numeric, conversion in the C: statement will not be possible and an error message such as "Cannot evaluate the expression" will appear when there is an attempt to use the contents of $string as though it held a number. Further conversion back to character form takes place within the final T: statement.

For a look at the reverse case, the following demonstrates conversion from a numeric variable to a string variable.

```
list
t: Type a number
a: #n
c: $string=#n
t: n= $string
```

Here the answer is accepted as a numeric variable and the PILOT system requires that it be entered as a number in the acceptable range for what the system can handle. If the input is not numeric, an error message such as "Numeric response required" will appear.

The general rule is that the C: statement first carries out any substitutions of #X or $string elements on the right side of the equal sign and connects them together with literal elements, performed in the same manner as the T: statement. If the left side is a string variable, the resulting character string is stored under that name. If the left side is a numeric variable, the right side is treated as a numeric expression to be evaluated, with the result stored under the numeric variable name.

CONVERSION FROM NUMERIC TO WRITTEN FORM

A further interesting conversion for reporting results is changing a numeric quantity to written form, just as one might write out the dollar amount on a check. As one application, a user of PILOT wished to present results in spoken form using a Votrax "Type-N-Talk"(tm) device. This device converts single digits to spoken form, but spells out "37" as "three, seven" rather than the desired "thirty-seven." The following PILOT program was designed to convert all but single digits to a written form that creates proper speech.

```
list
   R: Conversion from numeric to written form
   R: By A. Fejfar
*LOOP
T:ENTER A NUMBER, OR ZERO TO QUIT.
:
A:#Z
E(Z=0):
U:SAYNUM
J:LOOP
```

```
*SAYNUM
T(Z<10):#Z
E(Z<10):
J(Z>999):  THOU
J(Z>99):  HUND
J(Z>19):  TWENTY
T(Z=10):  TEN
T(Z=11):  ELEVEN
T(Z=12):  TWELVE
T(Z=13):  THIRTEEN
T(Z=14):  FOURTEEN
T(Z=15):  FIFTEEN
T(Z=16):  SIXTEEN
T(Z=17):  SEVENTEEN
T(Z=18):  EIGHTEEN
T(Z=19):  NINETEEN
E:

*TWENTY
C:Y=Z%10
C:Z=Z-Y
T(Z=20):  TWENTY
T(Z=30):  THIRTY
T(Z=40):  FORTY
T(Z=50):  FIFTY
T(Z=60):  SIXTY
T(Z=70):  SEVENTY
T(Z=80):  EIGHTY
T(Z=90):  NINETY
C:Z=Y
E(Z=0):
J:SAYNUM

*HUND
C:Y=Z%100
C:Z=(Z-Y)/100
T:#Z  HUNDRED
C:Z=Y
```

```
E(Z=0):
J:SAYNUM

*THOU
C:X=Z%1000
C:Z=(Z-X)/1000
U:SAYNUM
T:  THOUSAND
C:Z=X
E(Z=0):
J:HUND
```

For this application, it was not necessary to convert single digits to written form or to connect all the output together on one line. If you wish, you should be able to change the form of the digits with little effort. In place of the first T: statement that simply displays values of less than 10 in numeric form, you will need an array of T: statements, one for each specific digit from 0 to 9. If you wish to place the output on one line, it will be necessary to use C: statements to build up a character string that is displayed in one final T: statement. Here is how it can be done:

list
```
    r: Conversion to all written form on one line.
*LOOP
T:ENTER A NUMBER, OR ZERO TO QUIT.
:
C:$NUM=
A:#Z
E(Z=0):
U:WRITNUM
T:$NUM
J:LOOP


*WRITNUM
U(Z<10):UNITS
E(Z<10):
```

184

```
J (Z>999):  *THOU
J (Z>99):   *HUND
J (Z>19):   *TWENTY
C (Z=10):   $NUM=$NUM TEN
C (Z=11):   $NUM=$NUM ELEVEN
C (Z=12):   $NUM=$NUM TWELVE
C (Z=13):   $NUM=$NUM THIRTEEN
C (Z=14):   $NUM=$NUM FOURTEEN
C (Z=15):   $NUM=$NUM FIFTEEN
C (Z=16):   $NUM=$NUM SIXTEEN
C (Z=17):   $NUM=$NUM SEVENTEEN
C (Z=18):   $NUM=$NUM EIGHTEEN
C (Z=19):   $NUM=$NUM NINETEEN
E:


*UNITS
C (Z=1): $NUM=$NUM ONE
C (Z=2): $NUM=$NUM TWO
C (Z=3): $NUM=$NUM THREE
C (Z=4): $NUM=$NUM FOUR
C (Z=5): $NUM=$NUM FIVE
C (Z=6): $NUM=$NUM SIX
C (Z=7): $NUM=$NUM SEVEN
C (Z=8): $NUM=$NUM EIGHT
C (Z=9): $NUM=$NUM NINE
E:


*TWENTY
C: Y=Z%10
C: Z=Z-Y
C (Z=20): $NUM=$NUM TWENTY
C (Z=30): $NUM=$NUM THIRTY
C (Z=40): $NUM=$NUM FORTY
C (Z=50): $NUM=$NUM FIFTY
C (Z=60): $NUM=$NUM SIXTY
C (Z=70): $NUM=$NUM SEVENTY
C (Z=80): $NUM=$NUM EIGHTY
```

```
C(Z=90):$NUM=$NUM NINETY
C:Z=Y
E(Z=0):
J:WRITNUM

*HUND
C:Y=Z%100
C:Z=(Z-Y)/100
U:UNITS
C:$NUM=$NUM HUNDRED
C:Z=Y
E(Z=0):
J:WRITNUM

*THOU
C:X=Z%1000
C:Z=(Z-X)/1000
U:WRITNUM
C:$NUM=$NUM THOUSAND
C:Z=X
E(Z=0):
J:HUND
```

KEEPING TRACK OF PROGRESS IN A CLASS

The following program will give you some ideas to explore and build upon if you are interested in using PILOT to maintain information about the status of individual students in a class. A data file contains a list of student names, each followed by the number of the last completed lesson. Entry of a student's name that is already on the list results in display of the next lesson number for that student. If a student enters a name not found on the list, the new name is added to the list with an indication that no lessons have been completed.

```
list
r: CLASLIST copies from oldfile.txt to newfile.txt,
r: matches an entered name and returns next lesson number,
```

```
r: or adds new name and lesson #0 to the file.
r: OLDFILE.TXT must already exist and contain "zzzz" as
r:    an end-of-file mark.

openf: oldfile.txt,a
createf:newfile.txt
openf: newfile.txt,b
t:Please type your name.
a: $name

*next read:a
    m: zzzz
    jy:eof
    m: $name
    jy:found
    wr:b
    j:next

r: name not in file
*eof
    c: $newname=$name 0
    a: =$newname
    wr:b
    j:quit

*found
    c:n=$right
    c:n=n+1
    t:Lesson #n is next.
*finish
    wr:b
    read:a
    m:zzzz
    jn:finish
*quit
    rw:b,zzzz
    rewind:a
    rewind:b
```

```
*copy
    read: b
    wr: a
    m: zzzz
    jn: copy
    eof: a
    closef: a
    closef: b
    e:
```

Simulation of a
Problem Situation

The ability of PILOT to play the role of a conversational partner can be utilized to involve the user of your program in the solution of a realistic situation. Two examples are provided in this chapter. The first suggests how practice exercises can be developed for someone learning a foreign language. The second is an exercise for a student of medicine; it displays the invaluable advice of a programmed consultant who can offer comments about student responses.

AN APPLICATION TO
FOREIGN LANGUAGE LEARNING

Since I've emphasized the use of PILOT as a way to have your computer carry on a conversation, it seems reasonable to consider its application to conversation in another language. Why not? Pourquoi pas?

Most microcomputers made in the U.S. are not built to accommodate all the appropriate accent marks or special symbols used in some languages.

Meeting Someone

Many language texts begin with the rudiments of conversation; for example, phrases a traveler might need to deal with everyday situation. As an example, assume that you are a young man named Don Stewart who has been studying elementary French, and that you have just arrived in France, and are being met by someone you don't know. This brief program plays the role of someone sent to meet you, and you can practice your skills by responding. Unexpected responses will receive comments from an otherwise silent onlooker who is indicated by "*".

```
list
CH:
T: Assume that you are a young man named Don Stewart, that you
 : have just arrived in France and you are being met by someone
 : you don't know. You must respond when a woman approaches and
 : says:
T: Bonjour, monsieur.
A:
M: Bonjour
   TN: * A common response would be "Bonjour".
T: Etes-vous Monsieur Stewart?
A:
M: Oui
    TN: * Since you are playing the role of Don Stewart, you
       :  might say "Oui, je m'appelle M. Stewart."
T: Enchantee. Je m'appelle Jeanne Remond.
A:
M: Enchante
    TN: * Enchante means "Pleased to meet you."
```

With this beginning, perhaps you wish to elaborate the program to accept a student's own name, determine whether the student is male or female, and engage in a simulated conversation that would exercise language skills. The second stage of this conversation might go something like this:

```
list
CH:
T: This is an exercise in which you, an American, are being met
 : in France by Jeanne Remond, whom you have not met before.
```

    : Before we start, I need to know two things: your name, and
    : whether you are a man or woman.
    : What is your name?
A: $name
T: Thank you. Are you male or female? (type m or f)
*gender
A: $gender
CH:
T: Just after you pass through customs upon your arrival at the
    : airport outside Paris, a woman approaches you. She speaks
    : first, and then you answer. She says:
        R: Here we must decide whether our subject is male/female.
        M: f,female
        JY:female
        M: m, male
    JY:male
        R: What if neither male nor female is found?
        T: We'd better go back a few steps, $name.
        : Please tell me whether you are male or female.
        J: gender
*female
T: Bonjour, mademoiselle.
A:
M: Bonjour
        TN: * A common response would be "Bonjour".
T: Etes-vous $name?
A:
M: Oui
        TN: * You might say "Oui, je m'appelle $name."
T: Enchantee. Je m'appelle Jeanne Remond.
A:
M: Enchantee
        TN: * Enchantee means "Pleased to meet you."
J: end

*male
        T: Bonjour, monsieur.
        A:

```
     M: Bonjour
    TN: * A common response would be "Bonjour".
     T: Etes-vous $name?
     A:
     M: Oui
        TN: * You might say "Oui, je m'appelle $name."
     T: Enchantee. Je m'appelle Jeanne Remond.
     A:
     M: Enchante
        TN: * Enchante means "Pleased to meet you."
*end
     T: This is a temporary end to the conversation.
 E:
```

In this example, we not only make use of the student's name but ask whether the student is male or female because of the need to respond differently. Although the program asks for an entry of "m" or "f", we must realize that whether or not students understand, they may type something else. It is always good practice to have the program take care of all possible things that may happen. Thus, in this case, we arrange to repeat the question and jump back to accept the answer again.

The program is also written in a way that it accepts the responses of "male" or "female". These two words are potentially troublesome to distinguish because the sequence of characters in "male" is also contained in "female". Thus, if the program were written:

```
  . . .
M: m,male
JY: male
M: f,female
JY: female
  . . .
```

"male" would be matched in the response regardless of whether "male" or "female" were typed. The solution is either to look for "female" first or to be sure to look for a match with " male" instead of "male". Both were used above, but either one would have done the job.

Asking Directions

Another sample interaction might involve asking directions. We can prompt the student to either ask such questions or to respond to them. The computer can play the role of both the tutor and the respondent in French.

```
list
CH:
T: You have been sightseeing and need directions to return to your
 : hotel, Le Grand Royal. You decide to ask a policeman on the
 : corner. You say: (type your question)
A:
M: Ou
        TN: You might say "Où est l'hôtel Le Grand Royal, s'il vous
            : plaît?     The policeman would then answer:
T: Je crois qu'il est sur la place. Ce n'est pas loin d'ici.
 : Là-bas. (pointing)
A: Là-bas
M: Merci
      TN: It would be usual to say "Merci" or "Merci beaucoup."
T: This is a temporary end to the conversation.
E:
```

AN APPLICATION
TO MEDICAL INSTRUCTION

This example is a very different simulation in which the program user is asked to play the role of a junior physician who is faced with the need to diagnose a medical problem. A series of interactive programs along these lines have, in fact, been used as supplemental instruction in medical classes. You will once again see the close link between instruction and testing that occurs when conversational interaction is emphasized.

A program that attempts to recognize free-form responses is likely to become longer and larger as unexpected answers cause you to add further possibilities to the list of things the program must consider. Although program size was not a problem in the

194

example that follows, you can see that the program was divided into five sections. Only one section at a time needs to be present in the computer memory, and a new section is loaded when needed.

load
R: BEGINNING OF CASE7-GI DISTRESS
*C71
*ST
CH:
CA: 1, 20
T: ***   CASE 7
***
CA: 3, 10
T: ***   GASTRO-INTESTINAL DISTRESS ***
PA: 1
CA: 5, 10
T: CONTENT: WILLIAM THURSTON, M.D.
CA: 6, 19
T: ALAN BURKHALTER, PH.D.
CA: 7, 19
T: BERT KATZUNG, M.D., PH.D.
CA: 9, 10
T: PROGRAM: STEPHEN KORNBERG
CA: 11, 10
T: UNIVERSITY OF CALIFORNIA, SAN FRANCISCO
CA: 13, 20
T: JANUARY 1977
CA: 16, 14
TH: PRESS RETURN TO GO ON.....
A:
CH:
CA: 5
T: FOR THIS CASE, YOU WILL BE ON DUTY IN THE G.I. CLINIC.
PA: 1
CA: 7
T: (YOU MIGHT FIND IT USEFUL TO WRITE DOWN SOME OF THE
T: ESSENTIAL DATA AS YOU PROGRESS THROUGH THIS CASE.)

FOOT: PRESS RETURN TO BEGIN. . . . .
       R: /***** BEGINNING OF CASE 7 *****/
CH:
CA: 2

T: A FORTY-FOUR (44) YEAR-OLD WHITE MALE EXECUTIVE PRESENTS
T: YOU WITH A 12-MONTH HISTORY OF GNAWING EPIGASTRIC DISTRESS.
CA: 5

T: PAIN HAS BEEN PRESENT IN AN INTERMITTENT FASHION. THE
T: PAIN WHICH WAS ORDINARILY MOST SEVERE IN THE LATE MORNING
T: AND LATE AFTERNOON WAS TOTALLY RELIEVED BY EATING A MEAL.
T: THE PAIN WAS NEVER PRESENT ON AWAKENING IN THE MORNING.
FOOT: PRESS "RETURN" TO GO ON. . . . .
CH:
CA: 3

T: THE PATIENT TELLS YOU THAT THE PAIN WAS RELIEVED
T: COMPLETELY AND WITHIN FIVE MINUTES AFTER THE INGESTION
T: OF ONE OR TWO ANTACID TABLETS. ON QUESTIONING, THE
T: PATIENT VOLUNTEERS THAT HE WORKS LONG HOURS, SKIPS
T: MEALS, AND CONSUMES ALCOHOL ON A REGULAR BASIS. HIS
T: BOWEL HABIT HAS BEEN REGULAR AND UNCHANGED.
CA: 16

T: *** ONE MOMENT PLEASE ***
LOAD: CASE7-2

R: CASE7-2 (CASE 7-SECTION TWO)
*C72
CA: 16

TH: PRESS "RETURN" TO GO ON. . . . .
A:
CH:
C: B=0
C: C=0
C: X=0
C: Y=0
C: Z=0
CA: 2

T: PHYSICAL EXAM IS ENTIRELY NORMAL.
T: ROUTINE BLOOD COUNTS AND CHEMISTRIES ARE ALSO NORMAL.

CA: 5
T: THE MOST LIKELY DIAGNOSIS FOR THIS PATIENT IS. . . . .
T: (TYPE IN YOUR ANSWER)
C: A=4
*A1
CA: 8
CL:
A:
CE:
*ST
 R: /* MATCH ESOPHAGITIS */
M: ESOPH,
CY: Z=1
CY: A=A-1
J(A): *B1
J: *M8
*B1
JN: @M
CA: 10
T: PERHAPS. ESOPHAGITIS MAY BE PRESENT WITH EPIGASTRIC PAIN,
T: BUT IT IS USUALLY SUBSTERNAL IN LOCATION. TRY AGAIN.
J: *A1
*M2
 R: /* MATCH ATHEROSCLEROSIS-CORONARY ARTERIOSCLEROSIS */
M: ATHERO, ARTERIO, ASHD, HEART, CARDIAC, ANGINA, CORONARY,
CY: Y=1
CY: A=A-1
J(A): *B2
J: *M8
*B2
JN: @M
CA: 10
T: ALTHOUGH THIS PATIENT MAY HAVE CORONARY ARTERY DISEASE
T: AS WELL (ATHEROSCLEROSIS),   ISCHEMIC MYOCARDIAL PAIN IS
T: USUALLY RELATED TO EXERTION AND IS NOT RELIEVED BY ANTACIDS.
T: TRY AGAIN.
J: *A1
*M3

```
 R: /* MATCH ACUTE PANCREATITIS */
M: PANCREA,
JN: *M4
CY: X=1
CY: A=A-1
J (A) : *B3
J: *M8
*B3
CA: 10
T:    ALTHOUGH THE LOCATION OF THE PAIN IS PROPER, THE PAIN
T: OF ACUTE PANCREATITIS IS USUALLY OF SUDDEN ONSET,   MADE
T: WORSE BY EATING,   AND IS OFTEN ACCOMPANIED BY FEVER AND
T: VOMITING.   TRY AGAIN.
J: *A1
*M4
 R: /* MATCH DUODENAL ULCER */
M: DUOD,
C: B=1
JN: *M5
CA: 10
T:    CORRECT! THIS IS A CLASSICAL CLINICAL PRESENTATION
T: FOR A DUODENAL ULCER.
J: *S2
*M5
 R: /* MATCH GASTRIC ULCER */
M: GASTRIC,
C: B=1
JN: *M6
CA: 10
T:    POSSIBLY.   HOWEVER, THIS HISTORY IS CLASSIC FOR DUODENAL
T: ULCER. NO RELIABLE CLINICAL SIGNS OR SYMPTOMS EXIST TO
T: DIFFERENTIATE GASTRIC FROM DUODENAL ULCER IN A GIVEN PATIENT.
J: *S2
*M6
 R: /*PEPTIC ULCER */
MJ: PEPTIC, STOM,
CA: 10
```

198

T: CAN YOU BE MORE SPECIFIC ABOUT THE LOCATION
T: OF THE ULCER? WHY NOT TRY AGAIN?
J : *A1
 R: /*WHICH TYPE */
M: ULCER
JN: *M8
CA: 10
T: WHICH TYPE OF ULCER?
J : *A1
*M8
CA: 9
CE:
CA: 10
T: I'M SORRY, BUT I'M HAVING TROUBLE WITH YOUR ANSWER.
T: WHY DON'T WE LOOK AT A LIST OF POSSIBLE DIAGNOSES.
C: C=1
*S2
CA: 16
T: *** ONE MOMENT PLEASE ***
LOAD (C) : CASE7-4
LOAD: CASE7-3

R: CASE7-3   (CASE 7-SECTION THREE)
*C73
FOOT:
C: D=1
CH:
T: LET'S LOOK AT SOME ALTERNATIVE DIAGNOSES THAT YOU COULD
T: THINK OF IN THIS SITUATION.
CA: 4
T: COULD THE PATIENT HAVE.....
J (Z) : *P2
CA: 4, 28
T: ESOPHAGITIS (TYPE Y OR N)
INMAX: 1
CA: 6

A:

CA: 8

T: PERHAPS. THIS ENTITY MAY BE PRESENT WITH EPIGASTRIC PAIN

T: BUT THE PAIN IS USUALLY SUBSTERNAL IN LOCATION.

FOOT:

*P2

J (Y) : *P3

CA: 4, 28

CL:

CA: 5

CE:

CA: 4, 28

T: CORONARY ATHEROSCLEROSIS (Y OR N)

CA: 6

A:

CA: 8

T: ALTHOUGH THIS PATIENT MAY HAVE CORNONARY ARTERY DISEASE

T: AS WELL, ISCHEMIC MYOCARDIAL PAIN IS USUALLY CLEARLY RELATED

T: TO EXERTION AND IS NOT RELIEVED BY ANTACIDS.

FOOT:

*P3

J (X) : *P4

CA: 4, 28

CL:

CA: 5

CE:

CA: 4, 28

T: ACUTE PANCREATITIS (TYPE Y OR N)

CA: 6

A:

CA: 8

T: ALTHOUGH THE LOCATION OF THE PAIN IS PROPER, THE PAIN OF

T: PANCREATITIS IS USUALLY OF SUDDEN ONSET, MADE WORSE BY

T: EATING AND OFTEN ACCOMPANIED BY FEVER AND VOMITING.

*P4

C: D=1

CA: 16

T: *** ONE MOMENT PLEASE ***

200

LOAD (D) : CASE7-5
LOAD: CASE7-4

R: CASE7-4 (CASE 7-SECTION FOUR)
*C74
CA: 16
TH: PRESS "RETURN" TO GO ON.....
A:
*RPT
CH:
T: THE MOST LIKELY DIAGNOSIS FOR THIS PATIENT IS.....
CA: 2
T: (1) ESOPHAGITIS.
T: (2) ACUTE PANCREATITIS.
T: (3) GASTRIC ULCER.
T: (4) DUODENAL ULCER.
T: (5) CORONARY ATHEROSCLEROSIS.
*A3
CA: 8
CL:
CA: 8
INMAX: 1
A:
CA: 9
CE:
CA: 9
MJ: 1
T: PERHAPS. ESOPHAGITIS MAY BE PRESENT WITH EPIGASTRIC PAIN,
T: BUT IS USUALLY SUBSTERNAL IN LOCATION.   TRY AGAIN.
CA: 2, 3
T: XXXXX
J: *A3
MJ: 2
T: ALTHOUGH THE LOCATION OF THE PAIN IS PROPER, THE PAIN OF
T: ACUTE PANCREATITIS IS USUALLY OF SUDDEN ONSET, MADE WORSE BY
T: EATING, AND OFTEN ACCOMPANIED BY FEVER. TRY AGAIN.
CA: 3, 3

T: XXXXX

J: *A3

MJ: 3

T: POSSIBLY, BUT THIS HISTORY IS CLASSIC FOR DUODENAL ULCER.

T: NO RELIABLE CLINICAL SIGNS OR SYMPTOMS EXIST TO DIFFERENTIATE

T: GASTRIC ULCER FROM DUODENAL ULCER IN A GIVEN PATIENT.

CA: 4, 3

T: XXXXX

J: *E3

MJ: 4

T: CORRECT. THIS IS A CLASSICAL CLINICAL PRESENTATION

T: FOR A DUODENAL ULCER.

J: *E3

M: 5

JN: *Q1NM

T: WELL, THIS PATIENT MAY ALSO HAVE CORONARY ARTERY DISEASE,

T: BUT ISCHEMIC MYOCARDIAL PAIN IS USUALLY CLEARLY RELATED TO

T: EXERTION AND IS NOT RELIEVED BY ANTACIDS. TRY AGAIN.

CA: 6, 3

T: XXXXX

J: *A3

*Q1NM

CA: 16

T: *** TYPE THE NUMBER 1, 2, 3, 4, OR 5 ***

J: *A3

*E3

CA: 5, 3

T: *****

CA: 5, 25

T: -----CORRECT ANSWER-----

*E4

CA: 16

CL:

CA: 16

T: WOULD YOU LIKE TO DO THIS QUESTION AGAIN? (TYPE Y OR N)

CA: 16, 62

A:

M: Y

```
JY: *RPT
M: N
JY: *E5
J: *E4
*E5
INMAX: 64
CA: 16
CL:
T: *** ONE MOMENT PLEASE ***
LOAD: CASE7-5

R: CASE7-5  (CASE  7-SECTION  FIVE)
*C75
J: *ST2
*EN
CA: 16
TH: PRESS "RETURN" TO GO ON.....
A:
E:
*ST2
U(D) : *EN
CH:
T:    YOUR PRESUMPTIVE DIAGNOSIS IS DUODENAL ULCER. WOULD YOU
T: PERFORM THE FOLLOWING DIAGNOSTIC PROCEDURES  (TYPE Y OR N)?
CA: 4
T: UGI SERIES  (UPPER GASTROINTESTINAL-BARIUM X-RAY OF THE
T:              ESOPHAGUS,  STOMACH,  AND DUODENUM)
INMAX: 1
CA: 6
A:
CA: 8
T:    THIS PROCEDURE IS INDICATED. IT IS A VERY EFFECTIVE
T: DIAGNOSTIC TOOL,  SINCE OVER 95% OF PATIENTS WHO HAVE
T: DUODENAL ULCER WILL SHOW RADIOLOGIC EVIDENCE.
CA: 12
T:    ALSO,  OVER 90% OF GASTRIC ULCERS CAN BE IDENTIFIED
T: RADIOLOGICALLY.
U: *EN
```

CA: 4

CE:

CA: 4

T: ESOPHAGOGATROSCOPY (ENDOSCOPY)-DIRECT VISUALIZATION OF THE
T: G.I. TRACT WITH A FLEXIBLE FIBER-OPTIC INSTRUMENT.

CA: 6

A:

CA: 8

T: ALTHOUGH PROBABLY MORE RELIABLE IN DETECTING DUODENAL
T: ULCER IN MOST INSTANCES, THE EXPENSE AND COMPLICATION RATE
T: (ALTHOUGH SMALL) DON'T JUSTIFY ITS USE AS A SCREENING
T: PROCEDURE IN THIS CASE.

U: *EN

CA: 4

CE:

T: EKG (ELECTROCARDIOGRAM)

CA: 6

A:

CA: 8

T: THIS IS USEFUL IN EXCLUDING CASES OF ACUTE CORONARY
T: INSUFFICIENCY MIMICKING PEPTIC ULCER DISEASE.

U: *EN

CA: 4

CE:

CA: 4

T: SERUM AMYLASE   (A BLOOD TEST WHICH, IF ABNORMALLY HIGH,
T: SUGGESTS PANCREATIC INJURY OR INFLAMMATION.)

CA: 7

A:

CA: 8

T: THIS SHOULD BE DONE IN ANY PATIENT WITH ABDOMINAL PAIN-
T: ESPECIALLY OF RECENT ONSET—BUT IT WILL BE NORMAL IN THE
T: PATIENT WITH UNCOMPLICATED DUODENAL ULCER.

CA: 16

TH: PRESS RETURN TO GO ON.....

A:

CH:

T: YOU ORDER A UGI SERIES AND IT SHOWS AN ULCER CRATER

204

T: IN THE DUODENAL BULB.

CA: 4

T: THE PATIENT RETURNS TO YOUR OFFICE TWO WEEKS LATER. IN
T: THE INTERIM, HIS BUSINESS HAS SUFFERED AN ENORMOUS LOSS, AND
T: STOCKS HE HAS INVESTED IN HAVE SLID DRASTICALLY. HIS PAIN
T: HAS INTENSIFIED, AND NOW IT IS NOT ALWAYS HELPED BY HIS
T: ANTACID TABLETS, WHICH HE TAKES SPORADICALLY.

CA: 10

T: HIS PHYSICAL EXAM IS UNREMARKABLE EXCEPT FOR MILD
T: ABDOMINAL TENDERNESS.

INMAX: 64

CA: 16

T: *** ONE MOMENT PLEASE ***
T: *** TEMPORARY END ***
A:
E:

APPENDICES

Appendix I
History and Standards

THE HISTORY OF PILOT

The PILOT language developed as a result of experience with an interactive computer system called COMPUTEST[1], developed at the University of California in San Francisco in 1962. This system ran on a small IBM 1620 computer and was able to carry out interactive programs with one user at a time by means of its console typewriter. In early versions, the COMPUTEST system operated with program information (the program written in COMPUTEST) stored in a deck of punched cards and read into the computer a few cards at a time when the program was executed. Later, extended versions of the system had greatly increased capabilities by using disk-storage units that allowed random access to the program material.

When an IBM 360 model 50 computer with time-sharing capability became available at the UCSF campus, a new computer-assisted instruction system called PILOT[2] was developed. The language features of the PILOT system were patterned after those of COMPUTEST and stressed easy entry of instructional material by the program author. It was felt that a teacher should not have to become a computer expert in order to develop a computer-assisted instructional program. The PILOT system began to be used for traditional frame-oriented instructional programs as well as providing self-evaluation testing, practice with simulated clinical interviewing[3], and a number of applications that attempted to respond appropriately to natural language input from students[4].

Not long after the original version of the PILOT language was written for the IBM 360 computer, several versions of the language were programmed to run on other computers, some of them using more general-purpose languages such as BASIC, SNOBOL, PL/1, or an assembly language specific to the computer. Some were called PILOT, and some had derivative names such as PYLON and NYLON.

Partly because of the requirements of different computer systems and partly because of individual preferences, each version of the language was somewhat different from the others. In early 1973, representatives of six of the major versions of the PILOT language met together and agreed on a set of core language specifications to be common among all the systems. This language represented the experience of many workers in computer-assisted instruction at that time.

Recognizing that differences would undoubtedly arise, there was also agreement on a standard means of describing functions outside the core language. Because many of those involved had applications in elementary- and secondary-school settings, the resulting standard, called PILOT 73, was intended to be a language that would be easy for the program author to learn.

Although created prior to the availability of micro-computers, the Datapoint 1200 desktop computer provided a means to investigate self-contained operation and avoid the problems of communication with early time-sharing systems[5]. This machine had a built-in minicomputer, two magnetic cassette tape drives, a keyboard, and a cathode-ray tube for character display. The memory capacity of the first of these machines was 8000 bytes. About three-quarters of the memory was used for the PILOT system, leaving about 2000 characters of space for program material to be used at one time. This was enough to hold a number of instructional frames in active memory; additional material was read from tape when it was needed. The tape could contain about 100,000 characters of program material, and was sufficient for the development of modest adjunct elements of interactive instruction.

A major dialect of PILOT that departed from some of the PILOT 73 guidelines was developed by George Gerhold and Larry Kheriaty at Western Washington State College in Bellingham, Washington. It is called COMMON PILOT, and has extensions and additional functions to handle more complex programming needed in college-level instruction, particularly in mathematics and science. This version of PILOT has formed the basis of PILOT for the Apple microcomputer[6], for Radio Shack microcomputers[7], for C-Pilot on UNIX systems[8], and PILOT for the IBM Personal Computer[9].

PILOT 73 for the Datapoint computer became the basis of versions for an early microcomputer, The Processor Technology Sol. Before this company went out of business, it published a cassette version of PILOT, and a version for the company's Helios disk system was in preparation. These were distributed by PROTEUS, The Processor Technology User's Group[10].

The Atari company has developed PILOT for its microcomputer in a version that is easy for elementary students to use[11]. It contains graphic extensions providing the kind of "turtle" graphics found in LOGO. Although PILOT itself does not use line numbers, the Atari version requires them for program entry and editing, using the same mechanisms as provided for BASIC.

PILOT for microcomputers using the CP/M operating system was developed to provide the standard version for users of a wide range of equipment having disk storage. It is made available under the name Nevada PILOT by Ellis Computing in San Francisco[12].

REFERENCES

1. J. A. Starkweather, "Computest: a computer language for individualized testing, instruction, and interviewing," *Psychological Reports, 17,* 227, 1965.
2. J. A. Starkweather, "A common language for a variety of conversational programming needs," in *Readings in Computer-assisted Instruction,* H. A. Wilson and R. C. Atkinson (eds.) (New York: Academic Press, 1969) p. 269.

3. J. A. Starkweather, M. Kamp, and A. Monto, "Psychiatric interview simulation by computer," *Methods of Information in Medicine, 6,* 15, 1967.

4. M. Kamp, "Evaluating the operation of interactive free-response computer programs," *Journal of Biomedical Systems, 2,* 33, 1971.

5. M. Kamp, and J. A. Starkweather, "A return to a dedicated machine for computer-assisted instruction," *Computers in Biology and Medicine, 3,* 293, 1973.

6. "Apple Pilot" and "Apple Super Pilot," Apple Computer, Inc., 10260 Bandley Drive, Cupertino, CA 94017.

7. "TRS-80 Pilot," Radio Shack Education Division, 1600 One Tandy Center, Fort Worth, TX 76102.

8. T. Sumner, "C-Pilot Language Reference Manual," Alamonville, Ltd., P.O. Box 27186, Concord, CA 94527.

9. "PC/PILOT Language Reference Manual," Washington Computer Services, 3028 Silvern Lane, Bellingham, WA 98226.

10. "Processor Technology Pilot," PROTEUS, 1690 Woodside Road, Suite 219, Redwood City, CA 94061.

11. "Atari Pilot," Atari, Inc., 1272 Borregas Avenue, Sunnyvale, CA 94086.

12. "Nevada Pilot," Ellis Computing, Inc., 3917 Noriega Street, San Francisco, CA 94122.

EARLY STANDARDS FOR PILOT

The following are features required by the "PILOT '73" standards. These form a description of "core" PILOT as a minimal basis for the language.

Character Set

1. Alphabetic characters (A to Z)

2. Numeric characters (0 to 9)

3. Special characters ($"\ '\ (\ )\ \#\$\ .\ ,:;+-*\ /<>=?!@\ \&$)

Constants

1. Numeric constants: Core PILOT handles constants written as integers.

2. String constants: A sequence of alphabetic, numeric, or special characters.

General Statement Syntax

```
<PILOT STATEMENT> : : =
[<LABEL>] <INSTR> [<CONDITIONER>] [<RELATIONAL>] : [<OBJECT>]
```

1. LABEL (optional) consists of a name with the prefix *

2. INSTR (required) consists of a single alphabetic character for core PILOT statements.

3. CONDITIONER (optional) is a single alphabetic character Y or N appended to the PILOT instruction. The conditioner causes a test of the results of the latest attempted match (the most recently executed M-statement). If the conditioner is true, the current statement is executed; if the conditioner is false, the statement is skipped. The conditioner Y is true if the latest match was successful; the conditioner N is true if the latest match was unsuccessful.

   As an example, the statement "TY:HELLO" will display the word "HELLO" if an item of the last M-statement matches with an element of the last input accepted.

4. RELATIONAL (optional) is a conditional expression enclosed in parentheses and follows the PILOT instruction (and any conditioner). If it is evaluated to be true, the statement is executed; otherwise, the statement is skipped. The conditional expression is of the form: <numeric expression> <rel. op> <numeric expression> where rel. op (relational operator) refers to the symbols <, >, or = with the usual meaning for numeric expressions. Numeric expressions may be formed using the operators +, −, *, and /, interpreted as addition, subtraction, multiplication, and integer division, respectively.

   As an example, the statement "T(A>B):HELLO" will display the word "HELLO" if the value of variable A is greater than the value of variable B. "T(X):HELLO" will display the word "HELLO" if the numeric value of X is greater than zero.

5. The colon (:) is required.

6. The OBJECT portion of a statement follows the colon; its syntax depends upon the statement type.

Names and References

Labels begin with * and continue until the first blank. Labels must appear on a line and have at least one blank between the label and the code that follows. The label may appear alone on a separate line, as in the following:

```
*LABEL
T: DISPLAY THIS
```

Labels are used in the body of a J: or U: statement to refer to the place in the program sequence where the label occurs. Thus, J:*LABEL would cause a jump to the above sample program.

Core PILOT handles labels of at least four characters.

Numeric variable names are single letters of the alphabet. They are preceded by "#" when in the context of a character string. When a numeric variable name appears in the body of an A: statement, the input must be numeric. Its numeric value is stored and may be referenced by the name. Such references may appear in T:, Y:, or N: statements and cause the number to be retrieved and displayed.

```
A: #X
T: THE VALUE IS #X
```

Numeric variables are automatically set to a value of zero when the program is started. They may also be defined and set to a value by a C: statement that contains an expression such as Y=X-10.

String variable names begin with a "$". When a string variable name appears in the body of an A-statement, the text which is entered is stored and may be referenced by that name. Such references may appear in T:, Y:, or N: statements and cause the text to be retrieved and displayed.

```
A: $NAME
T: HELLO, $NAME
```

In the above example, if "ROBERT" is entered at the A:statement, then "HELLO, ROBERT" will be displayed.

A T:, Y:, or N: statement containing a string name without previously entered text will display the name.

```
T: THIS IS $UNKNOWN        will cause
  "THIS IS $UNKNOWN"       to be displayed
```

Core PILOT Statement Types

T (Type)

```
<T Object>          :: = [<T Argument List>]
<T Argument List> :: = <T Argument> [<T Argument>...]
<T Argument>        :: = <String Constant>
                    :: = <Numeric Variable>
                    :: = <String Variable>
```

The T: (Type) command is used to print text on the terminal. If the T Object is null (nothing after the colon), the statement produces an empty line. String constants are typed as is with no surrounding quotes. Variables are recognized by the variable prefix ($ or #) in the object. Variable names are terminated by the first nonalphanumeric character following the prefix. When a variable appears in the T Object, its name is replaced by its value. Items in the T Argument List are concatenated in the order in which they appear. For example:

T: HELLO $NAME, I UNDERSTAND YOU ARE #N YEARS OLD.

If $NAME = "FRED" and #N = 15, then the above statement would produce the following:

HELLO FRED, I UNDERSTAND YOU ARE 15 YEARS OLD.

Two additional forms of the Type statement are Y and N, which are exactly equivalent to TY and TN respectively. A colon by itself can be used for continuation lines.

A (Accept)

```
<A Object>          :: = <A Argument>
<A Argument>        :: = <Numeric Variable>
                    :: = <String Variable>
```

The A: (Accept) statement is used to receive input from the keyboard. The response is edited, replacing any or no leading and trailing spaces with one space at each end and compressing multiple spaces between words into single spaces. It is then kept in a buffer. If a variable name is present as an argument, the variable is set to the accepted value. In addition, many PILOTs provide a statement that can retrieve what is stored in a variable and place it in the accept buffer.

M (Match)

```
<M Object>              : : = <M Argument List>
<M Argument List>       : : = <M Argument>,<M Argument>,...
<M Argument>            : : = <String Constant>
                        : : = <String Variable>
```

The M: (Match) statement is used to compare a list of items with the contents of the string buffer. For each argument, a scan is made of the accept buffer until a match occurs or the end of the string is reached. The match is successful if at least one argument was successfully matched. A match of any item causes a YES condition to be set and if no item matches a NO condition is set. Following statements ending in Y are obeyed only if the YES condition is set and statements ending in N are obeyed only if the NO condition is set.

Arguments are separated by commas and may be string constants without quotes or string variables. Multiple spaces in match arguments are compressed to single spaces before matching, and leading and trailing spaces are significant. A comma which terminates the last item is ignored but can serve to indicate the presence of a trailing blank or blanks.

J (Jump)

```
<J Object>        : : = *<Label>
```

The J: (Jump) statement is used to transfer control to the statement whose label is the J Object. If the label is on a line by itself, execution continues with the first statement following the label. The J Object may be a label name with or without the label prefix(*).

C (Compute)

```
<C Object>        : : = <Assignment>
<Assignment>      : : = <Variable> = <Expression>
```

The C: (Compute) statement is used to assign values to numeric and string variables. The C: statement was designed as one means of extending the language, and specific syntax was left undefined so that it might match that of an available general-purpose language. Extensions of PILOT have in general followed BASIC-like syntax. Some have required prefixes to denote type for all variables and some have required this only for string variables, allowing statements such as "C:X=A+B". The concatenation and assignment of string variables allows the development of responses that make use of elements of user interaction

U (Use)

```
<U Object>      : : = *<Label>
```

The U: (Use) statement transfers control to the subroutine whose first statement is labeled with the U Object. The Use statement pushes the return location onto a push-down stack of at least seven levels.

E (End)

The E: (End) statement is used to return from a subroutine or to terminate the PILOT program. The E: statement pops the push-down stack, removing the return location from the stack.

R (Remark)

```
<R Object>      : : = <Anything>
```

The R: (Remark) statement is used for any comments which the author wishes to include in the program. The statement is ignored during execution. R: statements may be labeled and may be the target of J: or U: statements.

: (Continuation of Type Statements)

A colon at the beginning of any line will continue the object part of the preceding statement only if it was a Type statement (T, Y, or N). Labels, conditioners, and relationals are not allowed on continuation lines. If a conditioner or relational prevents execution of a statement, none of its continuation lines will be executed.

217

Additions Often Made to Core PILOT

While core statement types were to use single letters, it was expected that the language would be extended by the addition of other multi-letter names for new functions. This would indicate that they might not be the same in different versions of PILOT. Some common additions are the following:

Cursor and screen controls:

CA:	Cursor address to set row and column
CH:	Clear and home
CL:	Clear to end of line
CE:	Clear to end of screen

Various other aids to conversation:

FOOT:	Foot of screen halt and prompt
PA:	Pause
VNEW:	New Variables
XI:	Execute Immediate
CALL:	Call existing program
XS:	Execute from the system

The FOOT: statement places a prompting line at the bottom of the screen and waits for a response before proceeding.

The PA: (or PAUSE) statement halts program operation for a specified length of time, and then continues.

The VNEW: statement erases string or numeric variables.

The XI: statement obeys the contents of a string variable, which should be a valid PILOT statement. Such a string can be created as the result of prior interaction.

The CALL: statement provides a way to call upon the operation of separate program that exists in the computer memory external to PILOT.

The XS: statement calls upon the computer operating system to initiate operation of another program. This can be a useful linkage in using PILOT for an interactive front end to other operations.

Most versions of PILOT have file management and data collection facilities with statement names that relate to the operating system in use. Recent versions have graphic facilities that depend on specific hardware.

Appendix II
PILOT Systems
Compared

Those who have developed PILOT for different computers and for different applications have made extensions to the core functions, at times not adhering to the original standards in all respects. Here we will compare the text-oriented features of three versions of PILOT that are widely used on small computers.

The three systems are:

Nevada PILOT—for all computers using the CP/M-80 (tm) operating system.

Atari PILOT—for Atari ™ computers

Apple PILOT—for Apple ™ computers

PROGRAM PREPARATION

Nevada. This system has a built-in visual editor for the creation of standard CP/M text files. The editor can be configured to operate on a variety of display terminals. Other available text editors may be used.

Atari. The PILOT system makes use of the same program entry and editing facilities as those used by Atari BASIC. It, therefore, makes use of line numbers for editing purposes, but these have no effect on the operation of PILOT. An Auto command causes the line numbers to be automatically supplied during initial entry of the program.

Apple. A special editor called the *Lesson Text Editor* is used to write a PILOT lesson. This editor has a run mode designed so that a program author can test its operation, but this is not the usual mode for student use. There are three other special editors for developing graphic displays, sound effects, and special characters. The Graphics Editor allows development of graphic displays that become integrated with the lesson to either redraw an image step by step or to present the image all at one time. The Sound Effects Editor allows development of a sound sequence that can be called upon in the lesson sequence. The Character Set Editor allows development of new characters or pictures corresponding to specific keys on the Apple keyboard. Instructions in the lesson enable these characters to be put into operation.

Where there are differences between versions in the management of text and numbers, we will indicate what changes, if any, will allow translation of one version of PILOT to another.

CONSTANTS

Numbers

Nevada: Integers from -32768 to 32767

Atari: Integers from -32768 to 32767

Apple: All numbers are "real," with six significant digits. They may be expressed as integers, decimal numbers, or in scientific notation.

Strings

Nevada: Character text.
Atari: Character text.
Apple: Character text surrounded by double quotes.

In the PILOT 73 standards, character strings are considered literal constants unless preceded by a "$" (string variable) or a "*" (label). In translating from regular PILOT to Apple PILOT, there may be string constants used in C: statements that would require the addition of surrounding quotation marks.

VARIABLES

Numeric Variables

Nevada: Features 26 numeric variables, designated by #A, #B, #C, and so on, up to #Z. Within a C: statement, the "#" is optional.

Atari: Features 26 numeric variables, designated by #A, #B, #C, and so on, up to #Z.

Apple: Numeric variables are designated by a letter or a letter followed by a digit, 0 to 9. In a T: or A: instruction, the name must be preceded by a "#" and followed by a space or by the end of the instruction.
By reserving space with a dimension statement (D), a numeric array variable can be created, and individual elements in a one- or two-dimensional array can be referenced.

In translating from Nevada to Atari PILOT, the "#" symbol must be inserted as part of the numeric variable names in C: statements if it is not already present.

In translating from Nevada or Atari PILOT to Apple PILOT, a space (which does not appear in the display) must be added after references in T: and A: statements.

In translating from Apple PILOT to Nevada or to Atari PILOT, the character plus the digit names must be replaced by single character names, and the trailing space may need to be removed.

String Variables

Nevada: String variable names begin with a "$" and are followed by up to ten characters.

Atari: String variable names begin with a "$" and are followed by up to 254 characters.

Apple: String variable names consist of a letter or a letter followed by a digit 0-9 and in turn followed by $. In a T: or A: instruction, the name must be preceded by $ and followed by a space or by the end of the instruction. String variables must have space reserved with a dimension statement (D:) before they can be used.

The Apple designations for string variables are derived from the version known as Common PILOT; they are a departure from PI-LOT 73 standards, which specify that string variable names should be multi-character names beginning with a "$".

In translating from Nevada or Atari PILOT to Apple PI-LOT, one must reduce the name to a character or to a character plus a digit name. In T: and A: statements, add a second $ followed by a space (which does not display) to the end of the name. In other contexts, such as C: or M: statements, the "$" must be placed at the end of the name instead of at the beginning. In addition, a dimension statement (D) must indicate the maximum string size to be allowed.

DIFFERENCES IN PILOT STATEMENTS

The PILOT "core" statements of T, A, M, R, J, U, C and E are present in all three versions, the variations having been noted in the handling of numeric and string variable names. The Apple version uses an exclamation mark instead of commas as the separator of items in the M: statement.

In the following listing, each statement or function will be followed by the name or names of PILOT versions that contain it.

Variants of the Core Statements

Y: (Nevada, Atari)	An abbreviation substitute for TY:.
N: (Nevada, Atari)	An abbreviation substitute for TN:.
D: (Apple)	Apple PILOT requires a dimension statement to reserve memory space for string variables and numeric array variables. There must be a D: statement for each such variable before it can be used. Although this requirement (and this statement type) does not exist in Nevada or Atari PILOT, these versions do not provide substring functions for string variables or arrays of numeric variables.

TH: (Nevada, Apple)	The cursor remains at the end of a typed line.
AH: (Nevada)	The cursor remains on the same line after an entry.
AS: (Nevada, Apple)	Accept a single-character response.
AX: (Apple)	Accept an exact response; no editing.
A:= (Nevada, Atari)	The contents of a string variable name following the equal sign is accepted as though it had been typed from the keyboard.
MJ: (Nevada, Apple)	If this match is unsuccessful, jump to the next M:
MS: (Atari)	Match with special strings. If this match is successful, set string variables as follows: $LEFT= Everything to the left of the matched item. $MATCH= The matched item. $RIGHT= Everything to the right of the matched item. *Note:* These are set with the normal M: statement in Nevada PILOT.
MS: (Apple)	Allow one-letter misspelling for a match.
JM: (Nevada, Atari)	Jump to one of a list of labels, depending on which item in the previous M: statement was successful.
RW: (Nevada)	Write a remark to a data file (see data file operations on page 225).

Aids to Conversation

PA: (Nevada, Atari)	Causes the program to pause for a specified time without action or response. The number following PA: is in seconds for Nevada and in 1/60 seconds for Atari.
W: (Apple)	Waits for a specified number of seconds or until a key is pressed.
XI: (Nevada, Apple)	Executes the contents of a string variable as a PILOT instruction.

XS: (Nevada)	Executes an instruction of the operating system (CP/M).
CALL: (Nevada, Atari)	Calls an existing machine language program at a known memory address.
POKE: (Nevada)	Changes the value of a single memory location to the value of a numeric expression.
PR: (Nevada, Apple)	Problem start, used as a destination for branching instructions. In Apple PILOT, it is also used to set a variety of control options.
VNEW: (Nevada, Atari)	Clears string variables, numeric variables, or all variables.
INMAX: (Nevada)	Sets maximum input line length.
FOOT: (Nevada)	Causes text after the colon to appear at the bottom of the screen and executes an A:

Program Loading and Saving

GET: (Nevada)	Brings a program into the program buffer.
LOAD: (Nevada)	Loads program and initiates execution.
XEQ: (Nevada)	Same operation as LOAD:.
L: (Apple)	Loads program and initiates execution.
LX: (Apple)	Same as L: with erasure of current variables.

Cursor Control

CA: (Nevada)	Sets cursor address to indicated row and column.
POS: (Atari)	Sets cursor position to indicated column and row.
AP: (Apple)	Accepts an X,Y point from game controls. Cursor positioning and screen control occurs via control characters in the T: statement.
CH: (Nevada)	Clears screen and home cursor.
CL: (Nevada)	Clears to the end of the line.
CE: (Nevada)	Clears to the end of the screen.
RL: (Nevada)	Rolls the screen (contents move upward).

DATA FILE OPERATION

There is no easy translation of data file operations because of the different approaches taken by the three versions of PILOT. This is due in part to differences in the operating systems under which each version operates and in part to the degree of user flexibility each tries to provide. A listing of the commands follows.

Nevada PILOT

WRITE: or WR: Writes text of a preceding A: statement to an open data file on a peripheral device.

RW: Writes the text expression following the colon to an open data file on a peripheral device (writes a comment).

READ: Reads data from a peripheral device to the accept buffer or to a string variable.

CREATEF: Creates a data file.

KILLF: Kills (removes) a data file.

OPENF: Opens a data file.

CLOSEF: Closes a data file.

EOF: Marks the end of a data file.

REWIND: Rewinds (restarts) a data file.

APPEND: Appends to existing data in a file.

Atari PILOT

WRITE: Writes the text expression following the colon to a data file on a peripheral device.

READ: Reads data from a peripheral device to the accept buffer or to a string or numeric variable.

CLOSE: Closes a data file.

Apple PILOT

FO: Outputs to an open data file from a string variable.

FI: Inputs from an open data file to a string variable.

FOX: Creates and opens a new data file.

FIX: Opens an existing data file.

The following are commands usually used in an immediate mode (without a colon).

Nevada PILOT

RUN	Runs the current program in memory.
LIST	Lists the current program.
SAVE	Saves the current program.
BYE	Exits from PILOT to CP/M.
NEW	Erases the current program.
INFO	Provides file- and memory-size information.
DIR	Provides a directory listing of disk files.

Atari PILOT

RUN	Runs the current program in memory.
LIST	Lists the current program.
SAVE	Saves the current program.
DOS	Exits from PILOT to the disk operating system.
NEW	Erases the current program.
AUTO	Automatically numbers lines of input.
REN	Renumbers program lines.
TRACE	Provides a trace of program execution.
DUMP	Provides a listing of current string variable contents.

Apple PILOT

After being written with the text editor, Apple PILOT lessons are run either from Author Mode or from Lesson Mode. The author selects the Run option from choices provided by the Lesson Text Editor. Lesson Mode is the expected method for a student, who is not given access to the editor and its options. These are:

NEW	Begins a new lesson.
EDIT	Reads in an existing lesson for editing.
RUN	Runs a lesson as the lesson will run in Lesson Mode, and also shows error messages.

PRINT	Prints a lesson on a connected printer.
DELETE	Deletes a lesson.
QUIT	Returns to the main menu, which offers a choice of editors or initializes or duplicates disks.

Other Features

Both Atari PILOT and Apple PILOT provide graphic- and sound-generation facilities that are not summarized here. Nevada PILOT provides functions that control playback from a video cassette recorder.

Appendix III
Glossary of
Technical Terms

The definitions provided here are not technical, and are quite brief, but should provide some insight into the kinds of concepts that are being described when these words and expressions are used.

ADDRESS. A unique number, label, or name for a location in computer memory.

BACKUP. A copy of a program or a file made in case something happens to the original.

BIT. The smallest element of data, representing binary choice by 1 (on) or 0 (off).

BUFFER. A temporary storage space set aside within the computer memory for a collection of possible items. A *program buffer*, for example, is space set aside for the information necessary to store a program.

BYTE. A collection of 8 binary bits, operated on as a unit, and with the capacity to store one character.

CHARACTER. May be a letter, a punctuation mark, a number, or a symbol. Note that *characters*, even those that represent numbers, are not involved in computations; that is, the symbol "3" plus the symbol "2" does not yield the number "5". A character is not a quantity but a representation. A *control character* is formed by hitting the control key and another key simultaneously. Some control characters function as commands and are not displayed on the screen.

CODE. A sign that is used to stand for something. A more specialized meaning of the word is: That sequence of instructions, in a computer language, that makes up a computer program or part of a computer program. When you write a PILOT program, you will be writing *code* which is translatable into activity by the computer.

COMMAND. A direct instruction to the computer. A *statement,* by contrast, is indirect: It is entered as a line in a program and initiates no immediate activity. Almost every "sentence" in the PILOT language can be used as both a program *statement* and as a direct *command.* The convention we will adopt for this is to use the word "statement," except in the context of immediate execution. (The commands that belong to the Pilot Editor are not part of the PILOT language, and always result in immediate execution.)

COMPILER. A program that translates a program written in a high-level language, such as FORTRAN, into the machine code for a specific computer. It creates a machine code (sometimes called *object code*) file, ready to run. PILOT does similar translation, but most versions of PILOT operate directly from the PILOT program, with translation occurring when the program runs. (See INTERPRETER.)

CONDITIONAL. A programming element that controls whether a particular instruction will be executed or not. In PILOT, a Y or N suffix to an instruction makes its operation conditional upon the result of the most recent M: statement. Also, a logical or *relational* expression in parentheses can control the execution of the statement.

CONSTANT. An item of data that has a fixed, or constant, value; for example, 32 is a constant.

CURSOR. The rectangle or blinking underline that is visible on the video display screen. It serves to show the screen position at which the next character will be displayed.

DATA. Information that is referenced and processed by a computer program.

DATA COLLECTION FILE. A FILE set up to store information that the computer receives, usually from the keyboard. A file is very different from a buffer in that 1) a buffer is a temporary storage area that exists only during the operation of a program, whereas a file (at least for our present purposes) is a more permanent record; 2) a file is usually recorded on some kind of device (for example, tape or disk) outside the "memory" of the computer, whereas a buffer does not exist, theoretically, when the computer is inactive; and 3) a file consists of saved information, whereas a buffer is a place where information can temporarily reside. Recording a file on an external device is called writing the file; retrieving a file from storage is called reading it.

DATABASE. A collection of related data, such as a file of names and addresses in a mailing list.

DISK STORAGE. Storage of programs or data on a rotating disk coated with magnetic material, such as iron oxide. Data is written and read by read/write heads positioned over data tracks on the surface of the disk. Portions of the data tracks can be addressed for selected read and write operations.

FILE. A collection of related information, usually named and referenced as a *unit*. Think of a file as a way of saving such a body of information for subsequent use. A file can contain a program, text, or data of various kinds.

FORMAT. Refers to the required form or structure of a PILOT statement.

EDIT. Modifying a FILE in any way, including typing it into the computer for the first time. The Editor is that program or that part of a program that enables you to use certain direct commands to edit a file.

EXECUTE. To run a program. When execution occurs, the computer follows programmed instructions.

HIGH-LEVEL LANGUAGE. A programming language, such as PILOT, FORTRAN, or BASIC, that is written with codes more meaningful and mnemonic for human users and more directly descriptive of the problem at hand than the numeric codes required by the computer.

INITIALIZE. In programming, to set initial values to one or more variables before entry into a loop where the values may be changed.

INTEGER. A positive or negative whole number; for example 5, -5, and 0 are all integers.

INTERPRETER. A program that translates a program written in a high-level language, such as PILOT or BASIC, into machine code for a specific computer that immediately runs at the time of translation. (See COMPILER.)

JUMP. An instruction that causes the computer to find the next instruction to be executed from a location other than the next sequential location.

LOADING. Reading into the computer the instruction set that makes up the program. You cannot execute a PILOT program that you have saved on disk until you have loaded it. In some systems, loading a program will also cause it to execute.

MEMORY. The storage area of the computer. One of the most important facts to remember about computer memory is that it is limited. It is possible for a program, or a data collection file, to be too large for the computer to accommodate. Using a buffer is one way of allocating a portion of memory.

MENU. A screen display of choices for further action from which the user of a program may make selections.

OPERATING SYSTEM. A set of software routines that control the execution of programs running on a computer and manage the input/output portions of these programs.

PROGRAM. A sequence of computer instructions required to solve a specific problem or respond in specific way. Used as a verb, program means to develop a computer program.

RELATIONAL. A relational expression in a PILOT program is a form of conditional that expresses the relation between two numeric variables. A > B (A greater than B) is a relational expression.

SOFTWARE. Programs that control the operation of computer hardware.

STRING (or CHARACTER STRING). A set of consecutive characters; for example, "DOG," "23," and "This is a sentence" are all strings.

SUBROUTINE. A program segment that performs a specific function and may be used by other programs and routines.

VARIABLE. A name to which different values can be assigned. The equation x = 3 causes a value of 3 to be assigned to a variable named x. Computer languages have rules for designating variables. (See CONSTANT.)

Appendix IV
PILOT Quiz Sessions

QUIZ INTERACTIONS—CHAPTER 2

run

This is a brief test of concepts in Chapter 2.
It is of course written in PILOT.
Only PILOT functions already discussed will be used.

When "READY" appears on the screen, it it likely that
you are in _____ mode. (Type the fill-in word)
immediate
That's right,
You are probably in immediate mode.

Press "RETURN" to go on.

When you are in immediate mode, what should you type
if you wish to see a list of immediate commands?

Type ?
Yes.
You should type a question mark.

Press "RETURN" to go on.

In the run mode, PILOT tries to follow instructions that have been stored in the program space. If there is nothing there, what would you expect to see displayed?
READY
Yes, you would see just the word "READY".

Press "RETURN" to go on.

If you see the message "*UNRECOGNIZED PILOT STATEMENT", it means which of the following (Type 1, 2, or 3).

1. An immediate command is not one of those listed when you type "?".
2. A line of text in the program space does not contain a colon.
3. The text displayed above the message is not a legal PILOT statement.

3
That's right.

Text that cannot be interpreted as a legal PILOT statement is displayed just above the message.

Press "RETURN" to go on.

What are direct instructions in immediate mode called?
commands
Correct.
They are called commands.
Instructions in a PILOT program are referred to as _____.
statements

That's right.
They are called statements.

Press "RETURN" to go on.

What is the command to display the contents of the program space?
list
Right.
The command is "LIST".

Press "RETURN" to go on.

If you write a PILOT statement like "A:$response" it means that you wish to store the answer that a user gives to the A: statement so that you can use it later in the program.
    Is that a reasonable expectation? (True or False)
True
Yes, it might be used in a statement like:
    T:I know that you earlier said $response.

This is the end of a quiz for Chapter 2.
READY
bye

QUIZ INTERACTIONS—CHAPTER 3

run
This is a test of some of the concepts in Chapter 3.
It is written in PILOT.
Only PILOT functions already discussed will be used.
At any time, you may give an immediate command to jump to
    another question or to the end by typing "\J:*Qn"
    (n= question no.) or "\J:END" and two carriage returns.
For example, if you wish to jump to question 5 you should type
    "\J:Q5" and then press RETURN twice.

234

What is one of the characteristics of PILOT core statements
that are used in all versions of the language?
They are just a single letter.
Yes, they are abbreviated to one letter followed by a colon.

Press "RETURN" to go on

The PILOT statement that will display whatever is typed after
   the colon is the _____ statement. Enter a single letter.
T
Right.

Press "RETURN" to go on

An A: statement can accept an answer and also store it as a
   string variable. A T: statement can make use of the stored
   answer.

Consider the sequence:
   T: What name would you like me to call you?
   A: $title

How would you write a T: statement later on in the same program
   in order to say goodbye to the user by name?
   Choose a number.

   (1) T: Goodbye, $title.
   (2) T: Goodbye, user.
   (3) T: Goodbye, $name.
   (4) T: Goodbye, title.
1
Yes, "$title" will be replaced by whatever name was entered.

Press "RETURN" to go on

The M: statement looks for a _____ with an element of the last
   answer.
   Type the missing word.

match

You answered "match".

That's what I was hoping you would type.

Press "RETURN" to go on

Which statement has NO effect on how the program operates?

The R statement

Right.

The R (remark) statement doesn't change program operation.
It lets the program author make comments about the program.

Press "RETURN" to go on

A J: statement MUST have something after the colon. (T or F)

T

Yes.

It must have the name of a label that marks another place in
    the program.

Press "RETURN" to go on

The U: statement lets you use a program segment
    (1) just once.
    (2) a preset number of times.
    (3) as many times as you like.

3

Correct, you can use it over and over.

Press "RETURN" to go on

An E: statement marks the end of a _____.
    More than one word is correct. Type one of them.

program

Yes.

The E: statement marks the end of a program module
    (subroutine, segment) or the end of the entire program.

Press "RETURN" to go on

What symbol must always be present in a C-statement?
An equal sign
That's right.

Press "RETURN" to go on

The C: statement evaluates an expression on the RIGHT or LEFT
  side?
right side
Yes.
The result of evaluating what is on the right side of the equal
  sign is then stored in the variable on the left side.

Press "RETURN" to see your score.

You answered 10 correctly out of 10 questions.
READY
bye

QUIZ INTERACTIONS—CHAPTER 4

run
These are some questions about the ideas in Chapter 4,
written in PILOT.
At any time, you may give an immediate command to jump to
  another question or to the end by typing "\J:Qn"
  (n= question no.) or "\END:" and two returns.

If you write "CA:5,12" on the line before a T statement, the
text that gets displayed will start on what line? **5**
and in what column? **twelve**
That's right.
The next display will start on line 5 and column 12.
Press "RETURN" to go on

Cursor addressing can be useful for fill-in questions.
It can cause an answer to be entered in just the right <u>column.</u>

Here you see one way that it can look.
Press "RETURN" to go on

If you write "FOOT: Study the above, then press RETURN", you
    expect everything after the colon to appear on the
    last line of the screen. Type the missing word.
Yes.
The text is displayed on the bottom line of the screen.
Press "RETURN" to go on

During the pause initiated by a PA: statement, can a user
enter information through the keyboard? (Y or N)
no
Right.
The keyboard will not accept entry during the pause.
We are now pausing for a few seconds, so you can try it.

You probably won't have much occasion to use VNEW:$ unless
you save a lot of text in string variables and run out of
memory space.
VNEW:#, though, might be useful before asking a new
numerical test question. Would it hurt anything to use it
in the middle of this sequence of questions? (Y or N)
yes, I think it would.
If you said YES you were on the right track, since VNEW:
would lose our count of questions and the number correct.
Press "RETURN" to go on

Assume that the variable $SAYIT has the contents:
    A: $NAME

Would the following be a legal PILOT statement?
    XI: $SAYIT
yes
Yes, it would cause the user's entry to be stored in
the variable $NAME.
Press "RETURN" to go on

238

If you wish to leave PILOT and execute another program
as though you were giving a command to the computer's
operating system, what is the PILOT statement that
will let you do it?
XS:
That's right
The XS: statement will exit PILOT and send information
to the operating system.
Press "RETURN" to see your score.

You answered 7 correctly out of 7 questions.

QUIZ INTERACTIONS—CHAPTER 5

run
These are some questions related to Chapter 5.

They are written in PILOT.
Press "RETURN" to go on
"CURSOR" refers to:
   1. someone who swears.
   2. a careless expression.
   3. a marker on a display screen.
   4. letters connected together.

Choose a number **3**
That's the best choice when talking about computers.
The following is an example of a brief **module**.

```
*MOVEUP
    R: Variables R and C are used for cursor position.
C: R=R-1
CA(R):R,C
E:
```

That's the right word.

PRESS "RETURN" TO CONTINUE

To move the cursor up one line, a program could use this
module with the statement "U:MOVEUP".
    Is that True or False ? (T/F)
T
Yes, as long as R was already at the cursor's line number.
Press "RETURN" to go on
In PILOT, a module begins with a **label** and ends with **E:**.
Very good, right on both counts.
Press "RETURN" to go on

A "STUB" is:
    1. a nickname for a stubborn person.
    2. a short and thick section of program.
    3. an ache in one's toe.
    4. a comment printed in place of incomplete program code.
    Choose a number **4**
Yes, that's what it often means among programmers.
Press "RETURN" to go on

The M: statement followed by JM: can replace a sequence of:
    1. M:
        JY:
        M:
        JY:
    2. M:
        JY:
        MN:
        JY:
    3. M:
        JN:
        M:
        JN:
    4. 1 and 2
    5. 2 and 3
    6. 1 and 3
    7. 1, 2, and 3
4
Right.

The sequences in both 1 and 2 can be replaced by M: plus JM:
The sequence in 3 does something else, responding to "nomatch".

That's all for this quiz. Press RETURN to exit.

READY
bye

Index

242